The Newborn Baby
MANUAL

Renee Kam

He, she and so on

In this book, for no particular reason, the mother is she, the father is he and the baby is she.

The Newborn Baby Manual by Renee Kam
Published in 2013 by
Jane Curry Publishing 2013
[Wentworth Concepts Pty Ltd]
PO Box 780 Edgecliff NSW 2027 Australia
www.janecurrypublishing.com.au

National Library of Australia Cataloguing-in-Publication entry

Author: Kam, Renee.

Title: The newborn baby manual: everything you need to know about breastfeeding, baby sleep and baby behaviour/Renee Kam.

ISBN: 9781922190369 (pbk.)
ISBN: 9781922190383 (ebook : epub)
ISBN: 9781922190390 (ebook : Kindle)

Notes: Includes index.

Subjects: Infants–Care.
Child rearing.

Dewey Number: 649.122

Cover image: Shutterstock
Cover and internal design: Deborah Parry
Printed in Great Britain by TJ International Ltd, Padstow, Cornwall

Contents

PART 6: Useful Resources 207

About Renee

Renee is an International Board Certified Lactation Consultant, a physiotherapist with an interest in women's health, a mother of two girls, and a volunteer breastfeeding counsellor with the Australian Breastfeeding Association.

She has conducted private antenatal baby education classes since 2008. She is passionate about providing accurate, up-to-date and in-depth antenatal education to expectant parents on breastfeeding, baby sleep and baby behaviour.

Acknowledgements

This book could not have been written if not for the wonderful support and encouragement of my husband, Brandon, my Mum and Dad, my daughters, Jessica and Lara, my mother-in-law, Jenny, father-in-law, Sid, and my dear friends Cath, Rachel, Mardi, Michelle and Lara – you are all my rocks.

For much of the knowledge obtained through the years I owe a big thank you to the Australian Breastfeeding Association, particularly the likes of Joy Anderson and Barb Glare, who have answered countless questions that I have posted on ABAChat. I also owe a big thank you to Dr Jack Newman who has answered many of my questions so well and so efficiently.

Photography and illustration credits

Thank you to those who have kindly provided photos or illustrations for this book.

Joy Anderson: page 155
Donna Geddes: page 34
Judy Gifford: page 55
Yvette O'Dowd: pages 151 and 152
Andrea Polokova: pages 44 and 67
Susan Shaw: page 157
Drew Anderson: pages 69 and 70
Medela Australia Pty Ltd: pages 149 and 150

What this Book is About

This book is for anyone who is expecting a baby or is thinking about having a baby. If you already have a baby, you will still benefit from reading it. You will learn what is normal in terms of baby sleep, baby behaviour and breastfeeding. Although it focuses on the first three months with a new baby but much of the information can apply to the later months.

Introduction

These days, there is so much said or written about solutions for baby sleep 'problems'. From co-sleeping to controlled crying (oops, sorry, is it now called 'controlled comforting'?), everyone seems to have a different solution to a baby sleep 'problem'.

Let's first define a baby sleep 'problem', which is different for everyone. A 'problem' for some parents is not necessarily a 'problem' for others. In line with this, 'Is she a good baby?' seems to be a common question for new parents. However, everyone has a different perspective on what a 'good' baby is. Is a 'good' baby one who is seemingly undemanding, listless and sleeps a lot? The truth is, such a baby is likely to be undernourished.

New parents can feel immense societal pressure these days. It seems you are doing something 'wrong' and that you are a 'bad' parent if you have a 6-month-old baby who is *still* not 'sleeping through' the night.

We really are missing the point here. Trying to *solve* baby sleep 'problems' becomes redundant once accurate and detailed education about normal baby behaviour and sleep, and understanding a baby's cues, have been learnt antenatally (and practised immediately post-partum). Once a baby arrives, parents are usually overwhelmed and exhausted, which is not a great time to take on new information. An understanding of normal baby behaviour and baby cues before a baby is born can enable parents to understand their baby and develop a harmonious relationship from the beginning, whatever that may entail for that parent-baby pair.

The World Health Organization recommends exclusive breastfeeding for babies to 6 months of age, and thereafter for breastfeeding to continue alongside suitable complementary foods for up to 2 years and beyond.[1] While fulfilling these recommendations does not necessarily define a mother's breastfeeding success, the recommendations themselves are based on rigorous scientific evidence and help children to reach their full biological potential. Successful breastfeeding means different things to different mothers. Some mothers may have a goal in mind about how long they wish to breastfeed; others may just want to wait and see how it goes. Many mothers' feelings about breastfeeding continue to develop.

Are mothers achieving their breastfeeding goal? It seems there is a strong desire to breastfeed; statistics from the Australian Institute of Health and Welfare (2011) [2] show that 96% of mothers start off breastfeeding. However, despite a desire to breastfeed, the statistics show a sharp decline in both full and partial breastfeeding with each month after birth. By 1 month of age, 56% of babies are fully breastfed. At 3 months, only 39% are fully breastfed, 27% at 4 months and 15% at 5 months. The rates of children receiving any breastmilk are 75% at 1 month, 70% at 3 months, 68% at 4 months, 60% at 6 months, 42% between 7 and 12 months and 7% between 19 and 24 months.

Why are breastfeeding rates dropping like this? Why are many mothers not achieving their breastfeeding goal? [3] The answers are no doubt complex and multifaceted. Obtaining accurate and in-depth antenatal breastfeeding education, developing support networks and a commitment to breastfeed are all part of the solution. All these can impact upon how long a mother breastfeeds.[4] Developing a commitment to breastfeeding includes seeing it as the biological and social norm for feeding babies and young children. Antenatal breastfeeding education needs to include advice for mothers about who to contact when problems/questions arise post-natally, so that the right advice is obtained at the right time, before any major problems arise.

Many parents find that 'problems' do arise post-natally, and often feel at wits' end, exhausted, confused and not knowing who to turn to or what to do. Well-meaning but conflicting advice from family and friends may add to their confusion. They may find that they simply do not understand their baby and feel that everything they do is wrong. When people ask 'Is she sleeping through?' or 'Is she a "good" baby?' or 'Are you *still* breastfeeding?', it is no wonder they feel their baby is 'different'. So visits to doctors begin, and frequently the result is an ineffectual diagnosis of gastro-oesophageal reflux disease, lactose intolerance or food sensitivity etc, which can lead to more problems. Not a great recipe to start parenthood, the most *exciting* time of your life.

So what is normal and what is not? Babies just eat and sleep, right? Well, speak to any new parents and I am sure they will tell you this is far from the truth. Raising a baby is both challenging and hard work, to put it lightly. If you think about it, raising a baby without antenatal education is absurd. Who would go into a job interview without preparation? Well, this is the most important job interview in your life, yet most of us go into parenthood almost completely blind. The only knowledge passed on seems to be throwaway lines such as 'Get all the sleep you can now' or 'You'll be right. When you get there your instincts will kick in.'

I hope this book forms one of the crucial steps in helping you understand normal baby behaviour and breastfeeding and sets you on a path to happy and fulfilling parenting.

PART 1

Reasons Why a Baby Might Cry

Babies cry to indicate a need. It is completely normal for
a young baby to cry when being undressed, during a bath, at
nappy changes or when the car or pram stops. All this will change
in the coming weeks/months as your baby becomes accustomed
to her environment. The following chapters describe cues that a
baby typically shows when
indicating a need.

Feeding Cues

One of the biological needs of a baby is to be breastfed. When a baby is hungry, she indicates that in these ways:

Early feeding cues
- Turning head to side with open mouth
- Licking lips
- Sticking tongue in/out
- Wriggling (moving limbs)
- Elbows bent up, hands clenched over chest and fingers/hands to mouth

Intermediate feeding cues
- Fussing (including squeaky noises)
- Restlessness (intermittent crying)

Late feeding cue
- Crying (typically a repeated 'neh' [1] sound)

A young baby may display all or a few of these cues, and those displayed in one instance may differ in the next.

Because crying is a late feeding cue, it helps to have your sleeping baby near you so you can detect the earlier cues (i.e. squeaky noises) rather than wait until she begins to cry.

A baby tends to settle into a breastfeed better when she is calm because it helps ensure that her tongue is relaxed, forward and down where it needs to be to feed effectively. If your baby has reached the crying stage, it can help to briefly try to settle her before offering a breast (e.g. some skin-to-skin contact on your chest, stroking her back in one direction and talking to her).

Tired Cues

Another need for a baby is sleep. A baby will show she is tired with these cues:

Early tired cues

- Nestling her head into your body (she may do this for the first month or so)
- Staring
- Clenched fists
- Sucking on hands
- Her body tenses up
- Jerky, unco-ordinated limb movements
- Disengaging (e.g. turning head away from a stimulus)

Intermediate tired cues

- Yawning
- Intermittent grizzling (see chapter 71)

Late tired cue

- Crying (typically a repeated 'owh'[1] sound) which worsens the longer a young baby stays awake

A young baby may display all or a few of these cues, and those displayed in one instance may differ in the next.

Crying is a late tired cue. In fact, when a young baby has reached the crying stage of being tired, she is likely to be overtired which makes it more difficult for her to settle. Putting her to sleep as soon as you see the first yawn can help make the road to dreamland much smoother.

Wind Pain Cues

Wind pain can be classified into two groups: upper wind pain, which is alleviated by the baby burping, and lower wind pain, which is not so easy to alleviate.

Upper wind pain

Upper wind pain is alleviated by putting your baby over your shoulder to try to get her to burp. A baby with upper wind pain may be a bit squirmy and may make 'eh eh'[1] noises. Sometimes a baby may become a bit squirmy at the breast and perhaps come off the breast before she has finished feeding because she needs to burp. Burping her will allow her to resume breastfeeding comfortably.

Lower wind pain

Young babies have immature digestive (and central nervous) systems. It takes a while for their digestive systems to get used to digesting even human breastmilk, the perfectly designed milk for a human baby. For this reason, it is common for young babies to display lower wind pain signs from time to time (see chapter 72 for more detail). When experiencing lower wind pain, a baby may:

- Be generally unsettled
- Hold herself tensely (e.g. pull her legs up to her chest/straighten her legs strongly)
- Make little audible gasps among wails (high-pitched cries where the sound 'eairh'[2] features)
- Have a bluish tinge around her mouth
- Grimace
- Go red in the face
- Arch her head backwards or forwards

These cues typically occur in waves, where your baby relaxes between bouts of pain. A baby with lower wind pain will not be able to settle to sleep on her own and needs your attention (see chapter 72).

Other Cues

Hot/cold

If a baby is too warm, she may look flushed and her forehead may feel warmer than usual. If a baby is too cold, her lips may appear bluish, her forehead may feel cooler than usual and she may have goosebumps on her limbs.

As a general rule, babies need one extra equivalent layer for sleeping than what you are wearing. Never cover a baby's head for sleeping. If in doubt, it is better for your baby to be too cold than too hot because overheating is a risk factor for Sudden Infant Death Syndrome.[1]

Bored/lonely or uncomfortable

If your baby is awake (and is not tired or hungry), and has been doing the same activity or been in the same position for a while, she may be bored. Try doing something different with her. Or if you have not been around for a little bit, she may just want you back. Or she may just be uncomfortable. Try moving her or checking her nappy to see if it needs changing. A baby who is uncomfortable will typically make the sound 'heh'.[2]

PART 2

Breastfeeding

Favourite quotes:

"If a multinational company developed a product that was a nutritionally balanced and delicious food, a wonder drug that both prevented and treated disease, cost almost nothing to produce and could be delivered in quantities controlled by the consumer's needs, the very announcement of its find would send its shares rocketing to the top of the stock market. The scientists who developed the product would win prizes and the wealth and influence of everyone involved would increase dramatically. Women have been producing such a miraculous substance, breastmilk, since the beginning of human existence."
– Gabrielle Palmer

"Human milk is not a food ... It is a highly specialised infant support system." – Dr Stephen Buescherr

SECTION A:
THE PURPOSE OF
BREASTFEEDING

Breastfeeding: The Norm

Breastfeeding is the normal way that all mammals, including humans, feed their young. There is nothing special or different about breastfeeding. Breastfeeding is not a lifestyle choice, a social creation or a personal declaration. It is a fundamental component of our species. Breastfeeding is simply what mothers do. All babies are born to breastfeed. They are not making a lifestyle choice to do so; they are simply following their psychobiological destiny. Breastfeeding is a fundamental human right. It is a biological norm. The World Health Organization recommends exclusive breastfeeding* for babies to 6 months of age, and thereafter for breastfeeding to continue alongside suitable complementary foods for up to 2 years and beyond.[1] The National Health and Medical Research Council recommends exclusive breastfeeding for around 6 months and then for breastfeeding to continue alongside complementary food until 12 months of age and beyond, for as long as the mother and child desire.[2]

Society often talks about the concept of choice when it comes to breastfeeding. The truth, however, is that breastfeeding actually chooses us. Breastfeeding is an important part of the reproductive cycle. It is the final stage in the conception-pregnancy-birth cycle. The breast is programmed to take over from the placenta once a baby is born. Wanting to breastfeed is not special or different. Breastfeeding is not a social creation; not breastfeeding is.

Breastfeeding is a cost saving for the family and the community. For the family, it eliminates the need to buy artificial milk and the associated baby-feeding products (e.g. bottles, sterilisers). For the community, it reduces the burden on health services because of the various health problems associated with artificial feeding outlined below.[3]

Breastfeeding is environmentally friendly and convenient: it produces no waste products, requires no packaging or sterilising, and is portable and ready to use at the right temperature, thus requiring no fuel for heating.

The Lactational Amenorrhea Method (LAM) is a family planning method that is recognised by the World Health Organization.[4] A mother can use the LAM and have a less than 2% chance of becoming pregnant when she:

- Is exclusively breastfeeding
- Is less than 6 months post-partum
- Has not resumed menstruating[5]

As you read on in the following chapters what you see will not be all that surprising when you understand what this chapter has described. After all, why wouldn't something that is normal to our species and that has occurred over aeons help each of us to reach our biological potential?

Needless to say, there is simply no comparison between artificial milk and breastmilk, and nor will there ever be.

*Exclusive breastfeeding means that the baby receives only breastmilk. No other liquids or solids are given – not even water – with the exception of an oral rehydration solution, or drops/syrups of vitamins, minerals or medicines.[6]

Risks Associated with Not Breastfeeding

Companies that manufacture artificial milk revel in the 'breast is best' mantra because it implies that artificial feeding is sufficient, adequate, safe, benign and a normal way to feed babies. When we use this language it implies that breastfed babies may potentially be healthier but that artificially fed babies do just fine.

However, since breastfeeding is the normal way to feed babies, breastfeeding must be the point of reference, the benchmark, against which alternatives are measured. And so, rather than referring to breastfeeding as having benefits, we should be referring to the risks associated with artificial feeding. Failing to describe the risks of artificial feeding deprives mothers of important decision-making information and undermines the importance of breastfeeding.

Not breastfeeding increases a child's risk of:

- Gastrointestinal and respiratory illnesses requiring hospitalisation[1]
- Type 1 diabetes[2]
- Sudden Infant Death Syndrome[3]
- Necrotising enterocolitis in premature babies[4]
- Asthma[5]
- Ear infections[6]
- Childhood leukaemia[7]
- Coeliac disease[8]
- Mental health problems (including hyperactivity,[9] schizophrenia in adulthood[10])
- High blood pressure later in life[11]
- Higher total cholesterol later in life[12]

- Type 2 diabetes later in life [13]
- Obesity in childhood and later in life [14]
- Allergic rhinitis [15]
- Eczema [16]
- Poorer cognitive development [17] and lower performance in intelligence tests [18]
- Tooth decay [19]

Mothers who have not breastfed have higher risks of:

- Breast cancer [20]
- Ovarian cancer [21]
- Type 2 diabetes [22]
- Rheumatoid arthritis [23]
- Osteoporosis [24]

Mothers who do not breastfeed also tend to take longer to return to their pre-pregnancy weight.[25]

For a more detailed breakdown of the risks involved with not breastfeeding, refer to the National Health and Medical Research Council's *Infant Feeding Guidelines* (2012).

Substances in Breastmilk

Ever-changing

Breastmilk varies from the beginning of the feed to the end of the feed, and from day one, to day seven, to day 30, and so on. It even varies from mother to mother, and from baby to baby. A mother's breastmilk is made as required to suit her baby, depending on the baby's age and needs at the time. For example, the mother of a baby born prematurely will produce a different type of breastmilk to suit her baby's special needs.[1] Artificial milk never changes.

Absorption

Every substance in human breastmilk is designed for human babies, and breastmilk is a living substance, coming directly from a mother to her baby. Hence, substances in breastmilk are readily absorbed by your baby in a far superior way to artificial milk. Breastmilk is very robust, meaning that even freezing, thawing and reheating still renders it the best nutrition for human babies (for more information see chapter 62).[2]

Carbohydrates in breastmilk

Lactose accounts for most of the carbohydrates in breastmilk. Lactose enhances calcium absorption and readily breaks down to simple sugars (i.e. galactose and glucose) to supply energy to a baby's developing brain.

Another important group of carbohydrates in breastmilk are oligosaccharides, which are just one of the substances in breastmilk that help protect a baby from infection.[3] They promote the growth of healthy bacteria in a baby's gut.

Fats in breastmilk

Of the fats in breastmilk, 88% are made from long-chain fatty acids, unlike artificial milk.[4] It is these long-chain fatty acids (e.g. omega 3 fatty acids, especially DHA) that are constituents of brain and nerve tissue, and are needed in early life for mental and visual development. Artificial milk contains less cholesterol than breastmilk[5] – this may make it more difficult for a non-breastfed baby to be able to metabolise cholesterol later in life and hence have a higher risk of heart disease.[6]

Proteins in breastmilk

Artificial milk contains much more protein than breastmilk. This is because many artificial milks are based on cow's milk which has much more protein than breastmilk. Nature designed breastmilk to have less protein so that human babies would grow slowly – well, slower than calves. Growing slowly and steadily is especially important for brain development. The experiences that shape the brain come from close human contact (e.g. between a mother and her baby). If human babies doubled their birthweight in less than 50 days (as calves do), and then continued growing, it would make it difficult for a mother to carry her baby and keep her close. Calves need to grow quickly so they can learn where to find the best grass in the meadow; baby humans need to learn how to interact with those around them.

When a baby is young, whey protein predominates in breastmilk. Whey protein is easier to digest. As a baby gets older and her digestive system matures, gradually more casein protein appears in breastmilk.[7]

Many of the proteins in breastmilk serve an immunological protective purpose, rather than a nutritional purpose. For example, lactoferrin, which has antibacterial, antioxidant and anti-inflammatory properties and enhances iron absorption; lysozyme, which has antibacterial and anti-inflammatory properties; antibodies, which provide an immune response to environmental germs.[8]

Beta-casein

Most artificial milks are cow's milk-based and contain predominantly casein protein. Beta-casein is one of the major caseins in cow's milk. Broadly, beta-casein may be present as either A1 or A2 beta-casein. A2 beta-casein has been referred to as the 'original milk protein' because it existed before a mutation affected the ancestors of modern European cows. This mutation led to the appearance of A1 beta-casein in these cow herds and gradually spread to other herds throughout the world, including Australia. Today most cows in Australia produce milk with a combination of A2 and A1 beta-casein.[9] However, A2 Milk™ contains A2 beta-casein, rather than A1 beta-casein, because it is produced by cows specially selected for their genes to produce A2 but not A1 beta-casein.

When A1 beta-casein protein is broken down in the digestive system, a substance known as beta-casmorphin-7 (BCM-7) is produced. A2 beta-casein does not produce BCM-7 during digestion. BCM-7 is an opioid (morphine-like) peptide (small protein). BCM-7 may play a role in the cause of heart disease, type 1 diabetes and Sudden Infant Death Syndrome.[10]

Beta-casein protein is naturally present in both human and cow's milk (including cow's milk-based artificial milk) and therefore BCM-7 theoretically can be produced by both when digested. However, human and cow's milk BCM-7 differ in structure. Human milk BCM-7 is less potent.[11]

If a breastfeeding mother drank A1 cow's milk it is possible that BCM-7 from it could be transferred to her baby via her milk.[12] Breastfeeding mothers can avoid this by using A2 Milk™ (available in some leading supermarket chains in Australia and New Zealand) or by consuming A2 type beta-casein from other mammalian milk (e.g. goat, sheep and buffalo).

More research is needed, but there certainly seems to be mounting evidence that cows should be bred selectively for their ability to produce the original milk protein, A2 beta-casein, rather than the A1 beta-casein type.

Other important substances in breastmilk

Breastmilk contains a host of other important substances such as:
- **Anti-infective components** (e.g. white blood cells, antibodies, oligosaccharides, lactoferrin, lysozyme) used by the immune system to identify and neutralise foreign objects, such as bacteria and viruses

- **Growth factors** which help with the maturation of the intestinal lining and probably other tissues in the body
- **Stem cells** which have a remarkable ability to develop into many cell types in the body. These may help treat disease and make human tissue
- **Hormones** which are chemical messengers that carry signals from one cell, or group of cells, to another via the blood
- **Enzymes** which are catalysts that support chemical reactions in the body (e.g. to facilitate digestion). For example, the enzyme lipase in breastmilk makes digesting fats easier
- **Nucleotides** which are chemical compounds that are the structural units of RNA and DNA and are important for energy metabolism [13]
- Any many more…

SECTION B:
HOW BREASTFEEDING
WORKS

Breast Anatomy

Inside a breast there is glandular (milk-producing) tissue, fatty tissue and milk ducts. There is an average of nine (range 4 to 18) milk duct openings on to the nipple. The areola is the circular area of coloured skin around the nipple. Montgomery glands are the little bumps which encircle the areola and which produce oily secretions that keep the areola and nipple lubricated and protected.

ANATOMY OF THE HUMAN BREAST

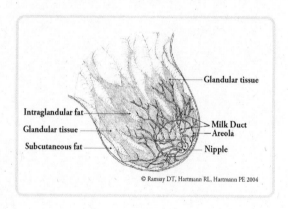

© Ramsay DT, Hartmann RL, Hartmann PE 2004

Breast Changes during Pregnancy

During pregnancy:

- The colour of the areola and nipple often darken
- The areola often enlarges
- Montgomery glands often become more prominent
- Veins along the breast surface often become more prominent
- Breasts often increase in size, as the glandular tissue grows inside
- The ratio of glandular to fatty tissue increases
- Breast tenderness is common and is a positive sign that pregnancy hormones are helping to prepare your breasts for breastfeeding

Breastmilk Production

During pregnancy

From about the fourth month of pregnancy, breasts start to produce colostrum, a thick, yellow substance that is rich in immune-promoting cells. High levels of progesterone during pregnancy inhibit colostrum from being secreted and keep the volume of colostrum 'turned down'.

Early breastmilk production

At birth, the delivery of the placenta results in a sudden drop in the level of the mother's progesterone which, in the presence of high prolactin levels, stimulates breastmilk production. Prolactin binds to receptor sites within the glandular tissue to stimulate breastmilk production. Other hormones (insulin, corticosteroid, growth hormone) are also involved, but their roles are not yet well understood.[1] Mothers typically begin feeling increased breast fullness (the sensation of milk 'coming in') about three days after birth. This is entirely driven by hormones at the time, meaning they occur whether or not a mother is breastfeeding.

This extra hormonal influence early on means that your milk supply is usually abundant for the first few weeks. This high hormonal drive early on creates the foundation for what your breastmilk supply will be like later. The more frequently your baby feeds early on (and therefore the more milk that is removed) will mean that your milk-producing capacity is greater for the entire course of your breastfeeding relationship with your baby. This is because frequent breastfeeds (and therefore milk removal) in the early weeks increase the number of prolactin receptor sites that are made within your glandular tissue, which in turn means that your milk-producing capability is increased for the length of time you breastfeed.[2]

Because of this heightened breastmilk production early on, some babies may refuse to drink milk from the second breast.

Supply equals need

After this time, this high hormonal drive pushing milk production ceases, and milk production is controlled entirely within the breast on a supply-equals-need basis. When milk is removed from the breast (the 'need'), it stimulates the breasts to produce more milk (the 'supply'). Although hormonal problems can still interfere with breastmilk supply, hormonal levels play a much lesser role in established breastfeeding. Under normal circumstances, the breasts will continue to make milk indefinitely, as long as milk removal continues.

It therefore makes sense that when you feed your baby according to her need (and she is feeding effectively – see chapter 12), she will receive exactly the amount of breastmilk she needs for her growth and development (i.e. she is in control of your milk supply). More frequent breastmilk removal means more breastmilk produced and less removal means less produced.

How do you know when your baby *needs* to feed? When she is showing feeding cues (see chapter 1).

Are a breastfeeding mother's breasts ever completely empty?

It is important for a breastfeeding mother not to wait for her breasts to 'fill' before feeding her baby. A breastfeeding mother's breasts are never completely empty. Breastmilk is continually being produced. In fact, your baby will drink an average of only 67% of the available breastmilk each feed.[3]

The more drained a breast is, the faster the milk is produced. The less drained a breast is, the slower the milk production. The reason for this is thought to be due to a small whey protein called Feedback Inhibitor of Lactation (FIL) in breastmilk. Milk production slows when the breast is less drained (and more FIL is present), and speeds up when the breast is more drained (and less FIL is present).[4] So, breastfeed your baby whenever she wants to be fed.

Also, the more drained a breast is, the greater the concentration of higher-calorie/higher fat-rich milk in that breast. The less drained a breast is, the greater the concentration of lower-fat/lower-calorie milk in that breast.[5]

There is typically more breastmilk in a mother's breasts in the morning, and gradually less as the day progresses. The fat content typically increases as the day progresses.[6] These observations are consistent with a fairly typical breastfeeding pattern of babies, whereby a baby gradually decreases the time between breastfeeds as the day progresses and has a longer sleep period at night.

To help ensure at least one breast is well drained at every second feed, it is helpful to alternate from which breast you begin a feed. This can help prevent blocked duct(s) or mastitis (see chapter 27).

After the first few weeks, a mother's breastmilk supply usually settles down to match her baby's needs; however, if the mother has an oversupply it may take longer (see chapter 15). Many mothers worry about their supply around this time because the feeling of fullness in their breasts diminishes and their breasts start to feel comfortable and soft. If you had previously felt your milk-ejection reflex (see chapter 11), you may begin to feel it less or not at all. If you express, you may notice that you are not getting as much milk. These changes are all perfectly normal. They just mean that your body has figured out how much breastmilk is being removed from the breasts and is no longer making too much. These changes may come about gradually or may seem to come on rather suddenly.

Of course, if a baby's needs change, a mother's milk supply can too. For example, if her baby needs more breastmilk, by feeding more frequently (thereby removing breastmilk more frequently) the mother's breasts will produce more milk (and vice versa).

Storage capacity

A mother's storage capacity (the amount of milk that a breast can store between feeds) is another factor that affects milk production. Storage capacity differs greatly between mothers and also differs between breasts of the same mother. The overall amount of breastmilk that a mother can make is not determined by her breast size, although breast size can reflect how much milk can be stored at any one time. This means mothers with either large or small storage capacities can both produce sufficient milk for their baby.

A mother with a larger milk-storage capacity may be able to go longer between breastfeeds without impacting her milk supply or her baby's growth. A mother with a smaller storage capacity will have breasts that fill up quicker and so she will need to breastfeed her baby more frequently to maintain her milk supply (by keeping her breasts well drained) and to satisfy her baby's needs.[7]

As an analogy, some mothers have 'shot-glass' storage capacities and others have 'beer-glass' storage capacities. A mother with shot-glass capacity will need to breastfeed her baby more frequently to meet her baby's needs, whereas a mother with a beer-glass capacity will not need to feed her baby as frequently.

Does my breastfed baby need any water?

Breastmilk is very thirst-quenching; it is about 90% water. Breastfed babies who are feeding well do not need extra water, even when the weather is hot and humid.[8] In such weather a baby often wants to breastfeed more frequently but for shorter periods. In this way she gets more of the thirst-quenching, lower-fat milk to help satisfy her thirst.

In fact, giving an exclusively breastfed baby any supplemental fluids can reduce her appetite for breastmilk and potentially reduce her mother's supply. It can also potentially have a negative impact on the duration of breastfeeding.[9]

11

Milk-Ejection Reflex

A baby's rapid sucking at the beginning of a breastfeed stimulates the nerve endings on the nipple and areola which in turn stimulate the milk-ejection reflex (previously known as the 'let-down' reflex). The milk-ejection reflex is where the hormone oxytocin acts on the muscle cells surrounding the glandular tissue, forcing the milk into the now expanded milk ducts towards the nipple. This results in a faster flow. The milk-ejection reflex occurs near the beginning of a breastfeed, after a few seconds and for up to a few minutes.

The first indication that the baby is getting her mother's breastmilk is when the milk-ejection reflex occurs. Before that very little milk can be released because breastmilk is not stored in the ducts.[1]

There are various ways a mother can tell when her milk-ejection reflex occurs. For example, some may:

- Feel a tingling in her breasts
- Feel a sudden fullness in her breasts
- Feel a slight pain in her breasts
- Feel thirsty
- Notice milk leaking from the other breast as the milk-ejection reflex occurs in both breasts simultaneously
- Feel a tightening in her lower tummy area, as oxytocin release also makes the muscles of the womb contract

Some mothers experience a milk-ejection reflex just by hearing or thinking about their baby. Some feel no symptoms. The only thing they notice is that their baby's sucking changes from shallow and quick to deeper and more rhythmical.

The milk-ejection reflex usually occurs multiple times during each feed in response to a baby's sucking. Most mothers notice only the first reflex (if they notice it at all).[2]

The milk-ejection reflex is a conditioned response mainly to a baby's sucking, but emotions also play a role. Factors that can slow the reflex include:

- Fatigue
- Fear
- Stress
- Anxiety
- Pain
- Smoking
- Alcohol
- Excessive caffeine intake
- Some medications

Some mothers find it difficult to stimulate a milk-ejection reflex when trying to express. This is because expressing cannot completely replicate how a baby suckles. Fortunately, there are many ways to try to help stimulate it (either for a breastfeed or when expressing). These include:

- Consciously trying to relax, using whatever method suits you (e.g. taking deep breaths, visualisation, meditation-type methods)
- Following a ritual before breastfeeding/expressing (e.g. having a warm drink, switching on the same music, then sitting in the same place)
- Expressing/breastfeeding in a quiet, warm, relaxing area, away from distractions
- Breathing slowly and deeply while expressing/breastfeeding
- Expressing/breastfeeding after a warm shower, or placing warm face washers on the breasts for a few minutes before starting
- Warming the breast flange (the part of the pump that goes over the breast) before expressing (e.g. with hot water or a wheat bag)[3]
- Gently massaging your breasts by stroking down towards the nipple, and gently rolling the nipples between your fingers just before breastfeeding/expressing
- Having your baby close by (or thinking about her or looking at a photo of her)

Nutritive and Non-nutritive Sucking

A baby sucking at the breast does not necessarily indicate that a baby is drinking (consuming) the milk. This is because there are two types of sucking done by a baby when at the breast: nutritive and non-nutritive. When a baby is doing nutritive sucking it means she is drinking the milk. When a baby is doing non-nutritive sucking it means she is not drinking the milk.

You can now see that the frequently advised 'feed the baby 20 minutes on each side' does not ensure a baby is getting sufficient milk. A baby who drinks very well (with lots of nutritive sucking) for 20 minutes straight, for example, will probably get a lot of milk. A baby who sucks non-nutritively for 20 hours will get very little milk and still be hungry.

When a baby comes to the breast, the first thing that must happen for her to be able to get the milk is for the milk-ejection reflex to occur in response to her sucking. This usually happens naturally and there is nothing a mother has to do.

It is normal for a baby to combine nutritive and non-nutritive sucking during a breastfeed. Typically she will start a feed with a lot of nutritive sucking, before moving between nutritive and non-nutritive sucking, with short rests. She will then either come off the breast or continue with non-nutritive sucking.

Non-nutritive sucking provides extra breast stimulation which can help a mother's supply, and there are many babies who find this type of sucking quite pleasurable. Breastfeeding is more than just the perfect nutrition; it is also very nurturing for a baby. There is nothing 'wrong' with letting a baby suck non-nutritively but it is important your baby is attached correctly to the breast to avoid nipple trauma.

You can distinguish between the two sucking actions by observation:

Nutritive Sucking

A baby who is nutritively sucking will drink with an 'open mouth wide → *pause* → close mouth' type of suck. The *pause* describes a pause in the baby's chin when it lowers to its lowest/widest point, just before the baby swallows. The pause indicates that the baby has a mouthful of breastmilk. The longer the pause in the chin, the bigger the mouthful of breastmilk the baby received. To demonstrate this to yourself, put your index finger into your mouth and suck as if you were sucking on a straw. As you draw in, your chin drops and stays down as long as you are drawing in. When you stop drawing in, your chin will come back up. See www.nbci.ca and watch the breastfeeding video clips (by going to the 'Information & Videos' section and scrolling down to 'Video Clips – English') to see babies demonstrating this type of sucking.

Non-nutritive sucking

When a baby is non-nutritively sucking and is not getting milk, her chin moves up and down rapidly with no pausing of the chin at the maximum opening. See www.nbci.ca and watch the breastfeeding video clips (by going to the 'Information & Videos' section and scrolling down to 'Video Clips – English') to see babies demonstrating this type of sucking.

Slow Flow of Breastmilk and Breast Compressions

Some babies respond to breastmilk that is flowing slowly either by falling asleep at the breast or by fussing (e.g. by pulling at your breast with her mouth, coming on and off the breast or by pounding at your chest with her fist). When this occurs, or when there is a concern about how much milk your baby is drinking, breast compressions can encourage your baby who is sucking non-nutritively to instead suck nutritively and obtain more milk. See www.nbci.ca and watch the breastfeeding video clips (by going to the 'Information & Videos' section and scrolling down to 'Video Clips – English') to see mothers using breast compressions.

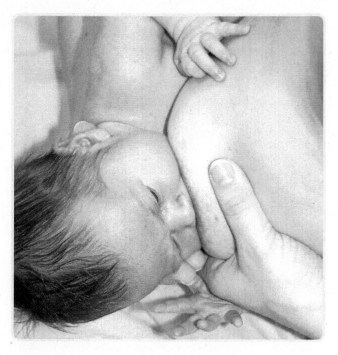

Breast compression

Breast compressions are achieved by:

1. Encircling your breast by placing your thumb on one side of your breast (e.g. the upper side) and your fingers on the opposite side (e.g. the underside) of your breast.

2. When a baby is sucking non-nutritively, compressing the breast to encourage the milk to flow into the baby's mouth (like simulating a mini milk-ejection reflex). Do not roll your fingers along the breast; just squeeze and hold. The compression usually gets the baby to start sucking nutritively again with the open mouth wide $\longrightarrow$ *pause* $\longrightarrow$ close mouth movement.

3. Releasing the breast compression when the baby either stops sucking or resumes non-nutritive sucking. This release allows the milk to start flowing again.

4. Repeating steps 1 to 3 above when the baby either resumes sucking (and the sucking is non-nutritive), or if the baby continues to suck non-nutritively after releasing the breast compression.

5. Continuing through steps 1 to 4 on the first breast until the baby no longer sucks nutritively in response to the breast compression. This usually indicates that she has finished drinking from that breast. However, let her remain on that side for a little longer because occasionally you may get another milk-ejection reflex which will make her start sucking nutritively again.

6. Allowing her to come off or taking her off and offering her the other breast if she is no longer sucking nutritively. Repeat the process on the other breast.

Bear in mind that using breast compressions during a breastfeed tends to be a temporary strategy. As a baby grows and becomes more skilful at breastfeeding, you will find that you no longer need to use breast compressions to achieve the same result.

Length/Frequency of Breastfeeds

Length of breastfeeds

Your baby's appetite should guide how long each feed lasts. Once your baby is satisfied, she is likely to detach herself.

The length of the feed really depends on how efficient your baby is at drinking, and also her age. A young baby is usually slower at drinking from the breast compared with an older baby. A baby who is on the breast and just nibbling (non-nutritively sucking) may spend an hour or so there without drinking much milk. However, a baby who is drinking well may spend 10 minutes on the breast and drink a lot of milk. A baby who is attached well to the breast is more likely to be an efficient and effective drinker.

Frequency of breastfeeds

It is common for exclusively breastfed babies to feed from a breast 11 times in 24 hours (range 6 to 18).[1] There is a wide range of 'normal' when it comes to the feeding patterns of breastfed babies and it is common for patterns to change, even within a 24-hour period. Most babies feed from one breast at some feeds and from both breasts at other feeds. However, some always feed from both breasts and others always from one breast.

The important thing is that a baby is fed according to her individual need (see chapter 10 under 'Supply equals need'). This will ensure she gets the number of feeds she needs (and therefore the amount of milk she needs, provided she is removing milk effectively).

As an analogy, if a baby needs to consume the equivalent of an entire pizza in a 24-hour period, it does not matter if there are eight or 16 slices. As long as she gets the whole pizza in 24 hours, she is getting what she needs, and she will get this if she is fed according to her need.

In 24-hour terms, it is common for exclusively breastfed babies to feed every two to three hours. The time between feeds is calculated from the time the last feed started, not ended. Commonly a baby has one longer stretch between feeds (usually up to five hours for a baby under about 6 weeks of age). It is also common for there to be one or two periods every 24 hours when a baby cluster feeds. Cluster feeds are where a baby typically has many feeds within a shorter period (e.g. three or more feeds within a few hours). For more information on cluster feeds (and unsettled periods) see chapter 72.

Can You Overfeed a Breastfed Baby?

(Contains information about oversupply and lactose overload)

In the true sense of the term, it is impossible to overfeed a baby who exclusively feeds from the breast. This is because a baby at the breast is in control of the milk supply – if she is hungry/thirsty she will do more nutritive sucking and when she is not she will either come off the breast or do more non-nutritive sucking.

On the other hand, when a bottle teat is in a baby's mouth, her reflex is to suck and she is unable to control the flow of milk from the teat (i.e. she is unable to non-nutritively suck). When a baby sucks on a bottle teat, she is likely to drink the milk whether she needs it or not (see chapter 43 under 'Nipple confusion' for more detail. Also see chapter 60 about how to pace bottle feeds).

Lactose overload

However, there is a benign condition called lactose overload which can occur in babies who drink an especially large volume of breastmilk because their mother has an oversupply (see below). When a baby has lactose overload, her digestive system has a bit of trouble handling the volume of breastmilk that she drinks. Lactose overload most commonly occurs in babies who are under 3 months; it is uncommon in an older baby.

The output from your baby's nappies is the most important factor in diagnosing lactose overload. A baby with lactose overload:

- Has a large output of urine (i.e. more than five heavy wet disposable nappies, or more than eight heavy wet cloth nappies, in 24 hours)

- Has many bowel motions, often with each breastfeed, which are often explosive, green and frothy; the breastmilk seems to literally 'go in one end and out the other'
- Is quite irritable between breastfeeds; many mothers say their baby is very 'gassy' or 'windy'
- Typically has adequate-to-large weight gains
- Often spits up quite a bit of breastmilk after feeds
- Will often not take a second breast when offered

Oversupply

A mother with an oversupply of breastmilk has an abundance that continues beyond the early weeks where it is normal to produce more milk than her baby drinks.

A mother with an oversupply tends to have:
- Rapidly filling breasts between breastfeeds
- Breasts that frequently feel hard, heavy and perhaps lumpy (but are relieved straight after her baby breastfeeds)
- Breastmilk which may leak from her nipples between breastfeeds

A mother with an oversupply is at higher risk of developing a blocked duct(s) or mastitis, so it is important to be aware of what the signs/symptoms of these conditions are (see chapter 27).

Fast milk-ejection reflex

A mother with an oversupply frequently also has a fast milk-ejection reflex. If so, she will often notice near the start of the breastfeed – when her milk-ejection reflex occurs – that her baby:
- Often gags or gulps
- May come off the breast coughing

Managing lactose overload, oversupply, and fast milk-ejection reflex

When a baby has lactose overload and a mother has an oversupply, steps can be taken to reduce the milk supply and settle the symptoms of these conditions.

Many mothers find 'block-feeding' helpful. Block-feeding slows a mother's milk production, which is helpful when she has an oversupply (or when a baby has lactose overload). Block-feeding means that a baby is fed from one breast only each block of time. The block of time depends on the degree of the lactose overload and the mother's oversupply. For some mothers a three-hour block of time may be sufficient. For others a six-hour block may be required. Block-feeding should be used only as a temporary strategy until the mother's oversupply/baby's lactose overload has settled.

A mother will know the block-feeding is working when she notices that her symptoms are settling (e.g. her breasts feel more comfortable more of the time) and her baby's output is settling (e.g. bowel motions are not quite as frequent, are less explosive/frothy and are changing more frequently to a yellow/mustardy colour rather than green).

When block-feeding, every time a baby wants a feed during this block of time, the same breast is offered. Then the other breast is used for the next block, and so on. This means that each time the baby comes back to the breast within the block of time, she comes to the breast that is more drained. She receives a lower-volume, higher-fat feed which can help slow the rate at which the milk goes through her digestive system.

Other tips for managing lactose overload:

- Keep the baby upright (e.g. over your shoulder) for a good 10 minutes or so after breastfeeds
- Place a wedge under the head end of the baby's mattress to elevate it about 30 degrees
- Avoid nappy changes or tummy time immediately after breastfeeds

Other tips for managing oversupply:
- Ensure that your baby is well positioned to breastfeed effectively (see chapter 24)
- Use techniques such as reverse-pressure softening (see chapter 19) or hand expressing (see chapter 57) to express a small amount of milk if you feel your breast fullness at the beginning of a feed makes it difficult for your baby to attach well

Managing a fast milk-ejection reflex:
- Breastfeed in a semi-reclined position. This can help a baby to achieve a better attachment and coordinate sucking, swallowing and breathing better
- Breastfeeding with your baby in more of an upright position can sometimes help her cope better with the fast flow
- If the above measures are unsuccessful, you may choose to trigger your milk-ejection reflex by expressing (e.g. into a cloth) before the breastfeed to catch most of the fast flow

You may find you need to do the above only for some feeds (e.g. the early morning one), or only at the beginning of feeds, as it may be at these times that your milk flows fast.

Note that all the above need to be tried over a few days before any significant change may be noticed.

It is reassuring to know that a baby with lactose overload and/or a mother with an oversupply and/or a fast milk-ejection reflex are temporary conditions. Most mothers find that by 3 months or so, things have settled down. When the problem is severe or ongoing it is worth consulting a medical adviser.

If you need more help with any of the above conditions, call the Australian Breastfeeding Association's National Breastfeeding Helpline, or seek advice from an International Board Certified Lactation Consultant (see chapter 75).

SECTION C:
EARLY BREASTFEEDING

Skin-to-Skin Contact

Breastfeeding has been the biological norm for feeding and nurturing babies since mammals first appeared.[1] A baby's ability to breastfeed is innate. She is born with instinctive behaviours, such as finding and grasping the nipple, attaching and beginning to suckle.[2]

The optimal time for a baby to initiate breastfeeding is within the first hour of her life, with skin-on-skin contact with her mother.[3] At this time, after an uncomplicated birth, the baby is typically alert and eager to breastfeed. Most mothers find that they cannot sleep after giving birth. This makes sense biologically as a mother's instincts are telling her to keep her baby safe. It has been shown in studies that early skin-to-skin contact contributes to longer-term breastfeeding rates, better maternal-baby bonding and more effective breastfeeding.[4]

Sometimes this skin-to-skin contact cannot happen immediately after the birth for medical reasons (e.g. breathing difficulties in the baby). However, this does not preclude successful breastfeeding. Whenever the initial skin-to-skin contact can occur, the benefits are the same, and it nearly always results in a baby instinctively seeking her mother's breast to feed. That instinct is reproducible for at least the first 3 months.[5]

There are many beneficial reasons for a mother and baby to enjoy skin-to-skin contact, particularly in the early weeks/months. Skin-to-skin contact teaches a mother to recognise her baby's early feeding cues, which can result in breastfeeding being easier and more relaxing. It also helps to initiate a baby's desire to feed by stimulating her innate feeding behaviours, such as tongue movements, putting her hands to her mouth and squirming in search of the breast.[6] Using her instincts, a baby can spontaneously attach to the breast with little or no help.[7] In these ways, skin-to-skin contact can help to lay down the foundation for breastfeeding.

It also helps to regulate a baby's body temperature, stabilise a baby's blood sugar level and heart rate, and reduce crying.[8]

Baby-Led Attachment

In modern Western society, a baby's instinct to find her mother's breasts can be disrupted by hospital routines, policies and procedures. This can lead to many mothers experiencing breastfeeding difficulties.[1] A newborn being separated from her mother, particularly in the early post-partum period, can be stressful for both and can result in breastfeeding problems. Forcing a baby to the breast when she is not ready to feed (as is often encouraged in hospitals by well-meaning staff) teaches her that breastfeeding is a negative experience, and is one of the main reasons a baby may have attachment problems and refuse the breast.[2]

Breastfeeding works best when mothers and health professionals adopt a supportive role in allowing babies to do what they are biologically hard-wired to do. When a baby uses her instincts to find her mother's breast, we call this baby-led attachment. Baby-led attachment usually ends in the baby achieving an effective attachment to the breast, thereby reducing the incidence of painful nipples and problems such as breast refusal or attachment problems.[3]

Baby-led attachment helps to get breastfeeding off to the best possible start when undertaken from the first breastfeed and at any other time, particularly within the first few months.[4] The more often a baby is allowed to find her mother's breast, the sooner she becomes oriented towards doing just that, and gradually all the steps a baby takes to find her mother's breast become more refined. When a baby knows exactly what she is doing, it becomes easier for the mother to adopt whichever position she likes to breastfeed in; the baby learns to easily and effectively attach to the breast no matter what the position.

The process of baby-led attachment may be described as follows:

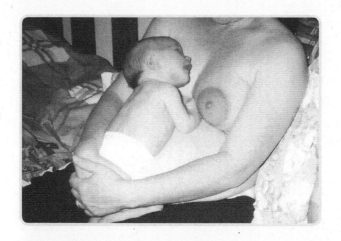

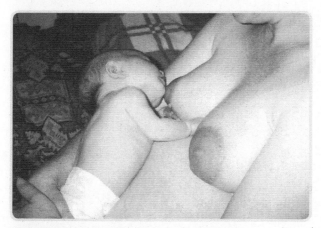

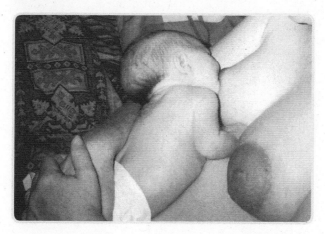

Baby-led attachment

1. Start with a calm baby (and a calm mother). For example, good times can be:
- As soon as your baby wakes
- When she is showing earlier feeding cues (see chapter 1)
- When she is in the active phase of her sleep (see chapter 68)

2. If your baby is upset, she may not be receptive. Things that can help calm her include:
- Talking to her
- Skin-to-skin contact
- Stroking her back
- Performing gentle rocking movements

3. Find a comfortable position with as much skin-to-skin contact as possible. Many mothers find that a semi-reclined position, with pillows behind them for support, works well.[5] A semi-reclined position lets gravity help the baby move towards a breast. In this position, your baby can be placed on your chest facing you, in between your breasts, with her head just above your breasts.

4. As your baby starts to instinctively move towards a breast, she will start to lift her head and bob it around. Different babies will bob, gently glide or even 'throw' their body towards a breast.

5. As she moves towards a breast, you may find it helpful to:
- Pull your baby's bottom closer to your body
- Provide support with your hand/wrist to her neck and shoulders

Avoid pressure on her head because she needs her head free to instinctively move it into a tilted back position to be able to attach effectively.

6. When her head nears your nipple, she may:
- Nuzzle around

- Lick and bring her tongue forwards (all of which are key aspects of breastfeeding)

7. When she finds the right position (well below the nipple) she will eventually:
- Dig her chin into your breast
- Reach up with an open mouth
- Attach to your breast

Aiming for your nipple to be lined up with your baby's nose when she does this can help achieve optimal attachment (see chapter 24 under point number 7 and under key points).

At this stage, a baby's instinct to suck is incredibly strong and usually begins instantly.

8. As your baby learns to follow through on her instincts and attach herself to your breast most effectively, it is possible that she may not attach perfectly. If you feel pain beyond the initial stretching of your nipple, your baby may not have taken a big enough mouthful of breast. You can break the suction by inserting a clean finger into the corner of her mouth, between her gums, and try again. Your baby may be happy to reattach without changing her position, or you may need to bring her more upright and restart the process. However, if she becomes upset or distressed during the baby-led attachment process, calm her and start again. This is a learning process for both of you so it is okay to take your time.

Key points:
- Start with a calm baby
- Find a comfortable position with as much skin-to-skin contact as possible
- Allow your baby to follow through on her instincts to find your breast and begin to suckle

Breastfeeding can take plenty of patience and practice. The whole journey can take days or weeks to 'click'. Starting this journey with lots of skin-to-skin contact and allowing your baby to use her instincts as frequently as possible to find your breast, can help you both to learn together how to breastfeed well. And, as the paediatrician and breastfeeding expert Dr Christina Smillie describes it, 'ooze confidence' that it will work.

See the following links on baby-led attachment:
- www.breastcrawl.org
- www.biologicalnurturing.com and see the 'Laid Back Video' under the 'For Mothers' section
- www.nbci.ca and see the 'Baby Led Mother Guided Started Upright Left Breast, Latches' video by going to the 'Information & Videos' section and scrolling down to 'Video Clips – English.'

For useful information regarding a plan for breastfeeding immediately post-natally, go to the Australian Breastfeeding Association website www.breastfeeding.asn.au and look for the article titled 'My Breastfeeding Plan'.

Colostrum

- Colostrum is the first breastmilk that a baby receives. It is a thick, yellow substance and is rich in immune-promoting cells, including antibodies and white blood cells
- Colostrum contains your baby's immune defence system for the first few days of her life
- Colostrum also contains plenty of long-chain fatty acids, protein (three times more than mature breastmilk) and fat-soluble vitamins (e.g. vitamin K and A). The extra protein in colostrum helps a baby maintain blood sugar levels. Vitamin K helps protect a baby against bleeding, and vitamin A is required for vision and is at its highest level in breastmilk for the first week
- Colostrum is richer in minerals and lower in carbohydrates than mature breastmilk
- Colostrum coats the lining of a newborn's digestive tract to provide it with a barrier from foreign substances. This reduces the risk of infection and possibly allergy, etc [1]
- Colostrum has an important laxative effect on the baby's bowel that helps remove meconium (the baby's first stool) from a baby's system

The combination of these concentrated nutrients, healthy bacteria and immune factors in colostrum gives the baby the healthiest possible start in life (also see chapter 61).

Normal Breast Fullness and Engorgement

Normal breast fullness

It is normal for a mother to feel a change in her breasts between days three and six after birth when her milk 'comes in'. When that happens the milk changes from the thick, yellow colostrum to a thinner, pale milk (often with a bluish tinge). A mother's breasts become larger, heavier and possibly tender or more sensitive. This normal breast fullness usually decreases within the first two or three weeks if the baby is effectively and frequently draining her mother's breasts.

Engorgement

Normal breast fullness may develop into engorgement between the third and tenth day after birth. With engorgement, the breasts are overfilled with milk and tissue fluid. The breasts can become painfully full, hard and swollen. They may appear shiny and have diffuse red areas. The mother may complain that her breasts are warm and throbbing (for more information see chapter 27).

The milk often does not flow easily from an engorged breast, and the swelling can make a mother's nipples become flat, making it very difficult for her baby to attach and suckle. In such a situation, hand expressing a little milk before attaching your baby can help (see chapter 57).

Alternatively, using a reverse-pressure softening technique can help. To do this, apply pressure with your fingertips at the sides of and close to your nipple, and then push inwards for 2 to 3 minutes, or until the breast tissue softens underneath. This softens tissue around the nipple and areola which can make it easier for a baby to attach. Many mothers find this technique most effective when lying on her back.

Some mothers suffer painfully engorged breasts, no matter how well and how frequently their babies are feeding. However, severe engorgement may indicate that breastfeeding may not be going well (i.e. that a baby may not be attaching and/or feeding effectively). If you are experiencing severe engorgement, seek advice from an International Board Certified Lactation Consultant (see chapter 75).

Although not as common, engorgement can also occur after breastfeeding is well established, such as when a feed is missed or when weaning is attempted too abruptly.

SECTION D: NIPPLES, AND POSITIONING AND ATTACHMENT

Do I Need to do Anything to Prepare My Nipples for Breastfeeding?

There is no scientific evidence to support any benefit to nipple preparation during the antenatal period. Antenatal treatment of 'inverted' nipples is not recommended because it has been found to be ineffective and associated with a negative impact on breastfeeding.[1] In a nutshell, there is no nipple preparation that needs to be done before breastfeeding; hormones in your body will naturally do all the preparation required.

Early Nipple Sensitivity

Nipples tend to be sensitive for the first 2 to 3 weeks post-natally. As a guideline, this sensitivity is typically felt for the first 10 seconds of a breastfeed, and then subsides. This represents your nipples becoming accustomed to a baby's sucking. If your nipples are painful at any time, or if your nipples start to show any signs of trauma (e.g. blistering, cracking or bleeding), it usually indicates that your baby is not attaching optimally, and it is advisable to seek prompt advice (e.g. from an International Board Certified Lactation Consultant or call the Australian Breastfeeding Association's National Breastfeeding Helpline, see chapter 75).

Causes of Nipple Pain

Nipple pain is the second most common reason why mothers abandon breastfeeding (perceived low milk supply is the most common).[1] With the correct advice and support, however, many mothers go on to have an empowering and successful breastfeeding relationship with their baby.

The most common cause of nipple pain in the early weeks is nipple trauma as a result of suboptimal positioning and attachment. Other causes include:

- Thrush
- Eczema
- Dermatitis
- Psoriasis
- Vasospasm
- White spot
- Bacterial infection
- Baby causes, such as incorrect sucking or mouth abnormalities (e.g. tongue tie)
- Incorrect use/fit of a breast pump
- Incorrect use/fit of a nipple shield

For more information on many of the above conditions, refer to section E.

Nipple Care

Do not use soap or anything that dries out your nipples. Do not scrub your breasts or nipples with rough towels after showering; gently pat them dry.

Ensure you obtain correctly fitted bras that account for your breasts enlarging throughout your pregnancy and during lactation. Maternity clothing stores which stock nursing bras, or Mothers Direct stores (in Melbourne and Brisbane – see www.mothersdirect.com), have trained staff to help correctly fit you. The best time to be fitted is from 4 months onwards in your pregnancy.

You will also need to purchase breast pads to soak up any milk (e.g. with a milk-ejection reflex – see chapter 11). You can buy reusable/washable breast pads, or disposable ones, or a combination. Some mothers use disposable breast pads when out and reusable/washable ones when at home. Remember to change breast pads frequently to ensure that your nipples are not in contact with damp pads because this can create a haven for some bugs.

Some mothers find it soothing to smear some breastmilk on to their nipples with a clean finger after each breastfeed and allow them to air dry before refastening their bra.

There is some recent research to suggest applying purified lanolin to your nipples after breastfeeds can help heal nipple trauma faster and reduce nipple pain.[1] Some mothers use this to help prevent nipple trauma in the early weeks too.

Positioning and Attachment

As mentioned earlier, skin-to-skin contact between you and your baby, and allowing your baby to use her instincts to find your breast, especially in the early weeks, helps get breastfeeding off to the best start possible. When a baby knows what she is doing, feeding becomes essentially baby-led attachment even if you are following the steps below; it is just that the mother has taken more control of the breastfeeding position.

Correct attachment of your baby to your breast helps her to feed well and also prevents nipple trauma.

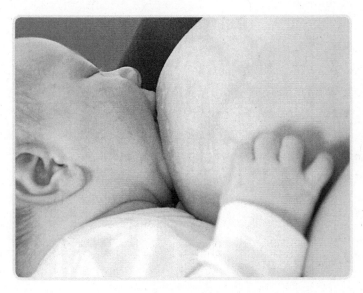

Good attachment

1. Start with a calm baby (watch out for earlier feeding cues – see chapter 1).

2. Unwrap your baby and hold her close.

3. Get comfortable; use pillows as required.

4. If using the cross-cradle hold position:
- Turn your baby on to her side with her chest and stomach close to you, her feet tucked around your side and her lower arm around your waist
- Support her neck and shoulder blade, rather than her head; your baby needs her head free to allow it to fall into its instinctive (tilted slightly back) position

5. Encourage your baby to open her mouth wide (e.g. by gently rubbing her lips against the underside of your nipple or areola). You may find holding your breast similar to a sandwich allows her to take more of your areola in, and makes it easier for her to attach.

6. Wait for your baby to open her mouth wide and for her tongue to come forward over her lower gum, and then pull her towards your breast, aiming for your nipple to be pointing towards the roof of her mouth. Your baby's chin should be her first contact point with your breast.

7. Your baby is attached well to your breast when:
- Her mouth is right over your nipple and covering a large portion of the surrounding areola
- She is covering more of your areola with her lower jaw compared to her top jaw
- Her tongue is down and forwards, cupping the breast
- Her chin is in, touching your breast
- Her nose is clear to breathe
- Her head is tilted slightly back
- Her top and bottom lips are curled outwards over the breast
- Her nose and mouth should be level with your nipple
- Her body is in close to yours

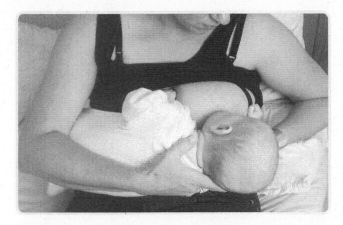

Cross-cradle hold

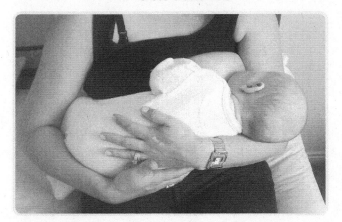

Cradle hold

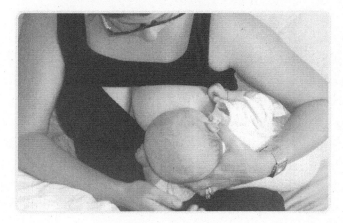

'Football' hold

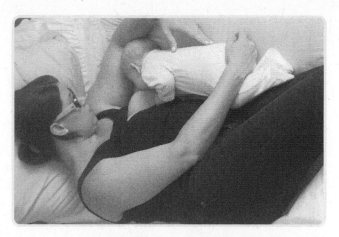

Side-lying position

Semi-reclined position

There are many positions that a mother can adopt to breastfeed her baby (e.g. 'cross-cradle' hold, 'cradle' hold, 'football' or 'underarm' hold, side-lying, semi-reclined, etc). There is no right or wrong position; it is a matter of finding a position that is comfortable for mother and baby and helps the baby get a good attachment, which in turn helps ensure effective milk intake. Take the time to try different positions to find what best suits. All the key aspects of attachment are the same for all positions and holds that a mother adopts. As you and your baby start to feel comfortable with breastfeeding, you will quickly learn to put her into the feeding position you have both come to enjoy.

Key points:
- Chin in, touching your breast
- Nose free
- Lips curled outwards
- More of the 'chin-side' of areola in her mouth than the side adjacent to her nose

Additional points:
- Your nipple should look round after a feed. If it looks squashed or creased your baby has not attached correctly
- It may be necessary to reposition your baby during a feed to maintain good attachment
- Breastfeeding should not be painful! Even if things look fine, the attachment may still not be quite right – it is how it feels that is most important. If it does not feel right, gently break the suction by placing a clean finger in the corner of your baby's mouth and begin again
- If you have any problems/concerns, seek help immediately (e.g. International Board Certified Lactation Consultant or Australian Breastfeeding Association's National Breastfeeding Helpline, see chapter 75).

What About Inverted Nipples?

Mothers who are concerned about their nipples would find it helpful to consult an International Board Certified Lactation Consultant (see chapter 75). Truly inverted nipples (i.e. where the nipples are completely adhered inwards) are rare. Some mothers can have flat nipples (ones that do not evert as far), however, which may take more 'coaxing' to come out. With some 'tricks' and persistence, most mothers with nipples of any shape or size can go on to breastfeed well. After all, it is *breast*feeding not *nipple*-feeding.

Some mothers find that:
- Pregnancy can help their nipples evert more, and more so with each subsequent pregnancy/breastfeeding relationship
- Using a baby-led attachment approach with lots of skin-to-skin contact helps their baby attach more easily
- If their breasts are particularly full or are engorged, their areola can become quite firm and make their nipples protrude even less. In this situation, implementing techniques to soften their areola before feeding (e.g. with a technique called reverse-pressure softening, or with some hand expressing) can help their baby attach more easily (see chapter 19 for more details)
- Temporary use of a nipple shield can help get a baby attach more easily. A nipple shield should be tried only after a mother's milk has 'come in' (see chapter 19), as the thicker colostrum is not easily transferred through a shield. And it should be used only after a face-to-face consultation with an International Board Certified Lactation Consultant (see chapter 75).

Most mothers find that breastfeeding gradually becomes easier and that their nipples begin to evert more easily as their baby becomes more skilful at feeding.

SECTION E: BREASTFEEDING CONDITIONS

If a mother is concerned that she has any of the breastfeeding conditions discussed below, a good starting point would be to call the Australian Breastfeeding Association's National Breastfeeding Helpline or consult an International Board Certified Lactation Consultant (see chapter 75). They can suggest appropriate management or advise who to see if necessary.

Painful Nipples

Some mothers experience painful nipples, mainly in the early weeks when mother and baby are learning how to breastfeed. The most common cause is suboptimal attachment. For many mothers with painful nipples, paying careful attention to positioning and attachment (see chapter 24) and smearing the nipples – using a clean finger – with breastmilk is enough to combat any problems.

Sometimes, however, other options may be necessary. For example, expressing (see part 3) for a day or two, or temporarily using a nipple shield (but only after a face-to-face consultation with an International Board Certified Lactation Consultant see chapter 75).

The following points can help maximise comfort when breastfeeding with painful nipples:

- Offer the breast with the least painful nipple first
- Stimulate your milk-ejection reflex (see chapter 11) before bringing your baby to the breast
- Try feeding your baby in a different position (e.g. semi-reclined)
- Apply a warm water compress for 5 minutes after feeds to help relieve pain [1]
- Some mothers find applying a moist wound-healing method (e.g. purified lanolin or a hydrogel dressing) between feeds helps reduce pain and hasten healing [2]

Engorgement, Blocked duct(s), Mastitis and Breast Abscess

Engorgement

With engorgement, the breast is overfilled with milk and tissue fluid.

Blocked duct(s)

A tender lump in an otherwise healthy breastfeeding mother's breast is probably caused by a blockage in one or more of the milk ducts. Milk can back up behind the blockage causing inflammation.

Mastitis

Mastitis is an inflammatory condition of the breast, which may or may not be accompanied by infection. The two main causes are milk stasis (where the milk is not flowing freely) and infection. Milk stasis is usually the primary cause, which may or may not be accompanied by (or progress to) infection. When mastitis is caused by, or has led to, an infection, it is referred to as infective mastitis. When mastitis does not involve an infection, it is referred to as non-infective mastitis.

Milk stasis occurs when milk is not removed from the breast frequently and/or effectively. For example milk stasis may be due to:
- Poor attachment
- Ineffective sucking
- Restriction of the frequency or duration of breastfeeds
- A mother having an oversupply of milk (see chapter 15 for more information on oversupply)
- Mothers who are breastfeeding more than one baby

Human breastmilk is not usually a good medium for bacterial growth and infection. This is because it has anti-infective substances which help ward off unwanted bacteria. However, unresolved milk stasis may result in the anti-infective properties being overwhelmed and creating conditions that are favourable to bacterial growth and hence infection. The presence of a nipple crack also has been reported as a possible entry route for bacteria.[1]

The clinical symptoms of infective versus non-infective mastitis are indistinguishable. In fact, the presence of pathogenic bacteria in the breastmilk does not necessarily indicate infection because pathogenic bacteria are often found in milk from mothers who do not have mastitis.[2] Deciding whether a mother has infective mastitis, and therefore requires antibiotics, or whether she has non-infective mastitis, is up to the discretion of a medical adviser, and requires a case-by-case thorough history and assessment. Typically, antibiotics are necessary if a mother's symptoms do not improve within 12 to 24 hours, or if the mother is acutely ill.[3]

Breast abscess

A breast abscess is a localised collection of pus. It is usually a complication of infective mastitis. Small breast abscesses can be aspirated with a small needle; larger ones may require a drain to be inserted or require surgical drainage.

Table of common features of normal breast fullness, engorgement, blocked duct(s), mastitis and breast abscess[4]

While blocked ducts, mastitis and breast abscesses are separate entities, in many instances they form a continuum where one can lead to the next.

The following table provides general information about normal breast fullness, engorgement (see chapter 19 for more on normal breast fullness and engorgement), blocked duct(s), mastitis and breast abscess. The table below is not designed to make a self-diagnosis. It is important to consult a health professional for an accurate individual diagnosis and management advice.

	Normal Breast Fullness	Engorgement	Blocked duct(s)	Mastitis	Abscess
When most commonly occurs (although can occur at any stage of lactation)	Between days three and six post-partum	Between days three and ten post-partum	Rarely in first five days post-partum. Most commonly in the first few months	In second or third week post-partum	In the first six weeks post-partum
Where typically occurs	In both breasts	In both breasts	In one section of one breast	In one section of one breast	In one section of one breast
Onset	Gradual	Gradual	Gradual	Sudden	Sudden
Signs	Breasts feel full, warm, heavy and hard. Skin remains soft and elastic (no swelling, shininess or redness). Milk flows well and baby able to attach and remove milk well	Breasts feel full, hard, tender and warm. Skin appears shiny and swollen with diffuse red areas. Nipples may be stretched flat, which can make it difficult for baby to attach and remove milk well	Section of a breast has a tender hard lump. There may be a patch of redness on the overlying skin. The affected area usually has little or no warmth	As for blocked duct(s) but more intense. The affected area is usually hot to touch	Extremely tender and hard lump with redness, heat and swelling of the overlying skin. There may be a thick, yellow pus discharge from the nipple. Ultrasound examination, or pus aspirated with a syringe, can confirm the diagnosis
Pain	May or may not have mild pain in the breasts	Throbbing or aching pain in the breasts	Mild pain in the area of the blocked duct, especially with the milk-ejection reflex. Symptoms are relieved as soon as milk is released from the blocked section of the breast	Intense pain in the affected area, especially with the milk-ejection reflex	Intense pain at the affected site

	Normal Breast Fullness	Engorgement	Blocked duct(s)	Mastitis	Abscess
Fever	No fever	Mother may have a low-grade fever (<38.5 °C)	Mother may have a low-grade fever (<38.5 °C)	Mother often has a fever (≥38.5 °C)	Mother often has a fever (≥38.5 °C)
Mother feels	Well	Generally well with breast tightness and discomfort	Generally well with tenderness in area of the blockage	Tired, aching muscles, run-down, feverish, and possibly nauseous*	Nausea, extreme fatigue, aching muscles, and fever*

*It is important to note that asymptomatic cases of mastitis or breast abscess have been reported.[5]

Treatment for engorgement

- Ensure your baby attaches well to your breasts (see chapter 24). Reverse-pressure softening or a little hand expressing may assist with this (see chapter 19 under 'Engorgement')
- Ensure your baby is breastfeeding effectively (see chapters 11 and 12)
- Alternate which breast you begin feeds from
- Do not restrict the length or frequency of breastfeeds, but rather feed according to your baby's need
- Avoid skipping breastfeeds or replacing them with other fluids (unless medically indicated)
- Gently massage your breast towards your nipple while feeding
- Use cold packs or cooked and then chilled cabbage leaves after/in-between feeds to relieve discomfort
- If necessary, express just enough for comfort after feeds
- Ask your medical adviser about pain relief medication if required

Treatment for blocked duct(s) and mastitis

As with all things, prevention is better than cure. Breastfeeding your baby according to her need, avoiding missed or restricted breastfeeds, wearing a well-fitted bra which does not constrict areas of your breasts and optimising your baby's attachment to your breast (see chapter 24) can help prevent a blocked duct(s) or mastitis.

When a mother has a blocked duct(s) or mastitis, frequent and effective milk removal is paramount.

If you notice any signs of a blocked duct or mastitis, you should:

- Apply some heat for a few minutes before breastfeeding (e.g. with a wheat bag or a warm shower)
- Loosen your bra or, even better, remove it during breastfeeds to prevent parts of your breast being squashed and hence potentially not effectively drained
- Feed first from the affected breast because this is the side that a baby tends to suck most vigorously at, and hence drain most effectively
- During the feed, gently but firmly stroke your breast with your fingertips, starting from the outer part of your breast, behind the blockage, towards your nipple. Some mothers find it helpful to perform this sort of massage, and some hand expressing (see chapter 57), after the breastfeed, perhaps while in the shower
- Use cold packs after breastfeeds for pain relief, and to help minimise inflammation
- Some mothers find that changing the positions they breastfeed in can help drain and unblock a blockage more effectively. For example, some mothers find that breastfeeding on all fours can allow gravity to help drain a breast (i.e. with baby lying on her back and the mother leaning over her baby)
- Rest as much as possible

When to see a doctor

A breastfeeding mother should contact her doctor immediately if she has any of the following symptoms:

- Flu-like symptoms (e.g. muscle aches, fever, chills, fatigue)
- A cracked nipple with obvious signs of infection (e.g. nipple may be red, hot to touch and thick, yellow pus may be present)
- Presence of pus or blood in your breastmilk

- Sudden and severe symptoms
- If a blocked duct is not cleared within 12 to 24 hours[6]

Since breastfeeding training opportunities in medical schools and post-graduation are limited, and because many doctors feel they require further breastfeeding education, it is important to be particular about whom you consult.[7]

Nipple Vasospasm

Nipple vasospasm is a condition where blood vessels in the nipples constrict and reduce blood flow to the nipple.

Features of vasospasm

- A sharp, burning or stinging pain in the nipples
- Nipples often change colour from a normal pink to white
- Nipples may change from pink to red to purple and then back again to pink [1]
- Nipples may alternate between colours (and types of pain) for minutes to hours [2]

Pain associated with nipple vasospasm often occurs in response to a drop in temperature, for example after a feed when nipples may suddenly be exposed to cold air. As blood starts to flow back to the nipple, it returns to its normal pink colour but the mother may still notice a throbbing pain.

While it is possible for nipple vasospasm to be an isolated condition, it most commonly occurs secondary to suboptimal attachment. It may also occur secondary to other conditions that cause nipple pain (e.g. thrush, bacterial infection). If the underlying cause is treated, the vasospasm should cease.

Also, medical problems such as Raynaud's phenomenon, a thyroid imbalance, rheumatoid arthritis or lupus are associated (and perhaps can cause) nipple vasospasm. [3]

Treatment for nipple vasospasm [4]

- Avoid cold in general (e.g. by keeping your entire body warm with warm clothing, a warm room, warm blankets)
- Cover the nipple as soon as your baby comes off the breast (e.g. with breast-warmers – breast pads which help maintain warmth,

see www.mothersdirect.com.au)

- Massage a little olive oil into nipples after feeds
- Avoid substances such as caffeine and nicotine that can cause blood vessels to constrict, as they can potentially precipitate symptoms of nipple vasospasm by reducing blood flow
- A dietary supplement with calcium/magnesium or vitamin B6 may help
- You may like to consult your medical adviser about a drug called nifedipine that can help improve blood flow

Nipple Infection – Is it Nipple Thrush or a Bacterial Nipple Infection?

When a breastfeeding mother experiences nipple pain, infection is the most likely cause when:

- She has nipple pain beyond the first week
- She has nipple pain/trauma which refuses to heal
- She has nipple pain after a period of comfortable breastfeeding
- Her baby is attaching well to her breast
- Other causes of nipple pain/trauma have been ruled out (e.g. eczema, vasospasm, mouth abnormalities in the baby, such as tongue tie)

The most common causes of nipple infection are thought to be caused by either nipple thrush (where a bug called *Candida albicans* is the culprit) or a bacterial nipple infection (where a bug called *Staphylococcus aureus* is the likely culprit). Both can present similarly making it difficult to determine which is responsible.

1. Nipple thrush

Features[1]

- A burning, itching, stinging or stabbing pain in the nipple
- Sometimes a sharp shooting or a deep aching pain which radiates into the breast is described
- The pain typically occurs after and/or between breastfeeds but can occur during the feed
- The pain may be present in one or both breasts
- The pain can be mild to severe

- Nipples are often very sensitive to touch
- The nipple may appear normal or may be brighter pink than usual
- The areola may appear red, shiny or have white flaky bits over it, and it may be itchy, although there may be none of these signs
- There may be white areas on the insides of your baby's cheeks or on her tongue, which look like milk curds and which cannot be easily scraped off
- Your baby may have a red spotty nappy rash

Factors that can predispose to the development of nipple thrush

Nipple thrush can sometimes seem to appear out of the blue, but there are certain factors which can predispose to this condition. These include:

- A recent course of antibiotics (e.g. to treat infective mastitis or other infections). This is the most common cause [2]
- A history of vaginal thrush
- A history of nipple damage

Treatment for nipple thrush

Consult your medical adviser immediately if you are concerned you may have nipple thrush. If it is diagnosed, an antifungal treatment is often prescribed.

If a topical treatment (e.g. with a cream) is not working, treatment often progresses to a systemic treatment (e.g. a medication).

The following links may be helpful:

- The Royal Women's Hospital (Melbourne) Breastfeeding: Thrush in Lactation clinical practice guideline (2004) which can be downloaded from: www.thewomens.org.au/ BreastfeedingClinicalPracticeGuidelines
- Dr Jack Newman's Candida Protocol (2009) which can be downloaded from: www.breastfeedinginc.ca/content. php?pagename=information

Treatment for thrush typically takes at least one week to be effective. Thrush is easily transferred between a breastfeeding mother and her baby, or vice versa. Therefore, many jurisdictions suggest that the baby be treated when thrush is diagnosed (e.g. with oral antifungal drops), even if asymptomatic, to prevent mother and baby passing it back and forth.[3] Treatment should continue until mother and baby have been symptom-free for several days.[4]

Recent research into ongoing, severe nipple pain suggests that what was once presumed to be thrush, but antifungal treatment was not effective, may represent a bacterial nipple infection (see below). This would be most likely if you have/had a cracked nipple and particularly if there is a yellow discharge.[5] So if you have been diagnosed as having thrush but the treatment is not working after a couple of weeks, consult your medical adviser again because it may indicate that a bacterial infection is present instead, and a different treatment may be required (e.g. an antibiotic ointment).[6]

Other tips when treating thrush

Not every case of nipple thrush is likely to need the following measures, but if it persists and other possible causes of the nipple pain have been eliminated, these may help prevent it being exacerbated or prolonged.

- Be meticulous about washing your hands before and after breastfeeds and nappy changes. Normal soap is better than antibacterial soap because helpful bacteria are important to help prevent *Candida* from thriving
- Seek advice from a dietitian about dietary changes that may help (see www.daa.asn.au)
- Wash/change your towels, breast pads, bras, etc frequently and hang them out in the sun[7]
- If using a dummy, replace and/or sterilise it frequently[8]

2. Bacterial Nipple Infection

Features

The following points may make the diagnosis of a bacterial nipple infection more likely:

- Nipple trauma with signs of inflammation (e.g. redness, swelling, heat and tenderness)
- A yellow discharge from the nipple

However, nipple infection may be the cause of nipple pain even when there are no obvious signs of trauma or inflammation.[9] This may be because the level of bacteria is enough to cause pain but not enough to cause any obvious signs of infection, such as the above. Nipples can be slightly damaged while being elongated during a breastfeed but not enough to show any obvious sign of trauma. It is not uncommon to hear reports from mothers of their baby spitting up milk mixed with some blood after a feed, even when the mother has no obvious crack in her nipple. In these situations it is often assumed that the blood has come from small hidden cracks which may be harbouring an infection.

Treatment for a bacterial nipple infection

Consult your medical adviser immediately if you are concerned that you may have a bacterial nipple infection. If that is diagnosed, an antibiotic treatment is often prescribed.

If a topical treatment (e.g. with a cream) is not working, treatment often progresses to a systemic treatment (e.g. a medication).

Combination therapy

Because it can be very difficult to discern whether the cause of a nipple infection is thrush or a bacterial infection, some, such as the paediatrician and breastfeeding expert Dr Jack Newman, advocate combination therapy using an antibacterial, antifungal and steroid cream.[10]

Important points to remember

There is no reason to stop breastfeeding if you have thrush or a bacterial nipple infection. If a baby has thrush in her mouth, she may continue to breastfeed normally, or she may be fussy or even reluctant to breastfeed. However, once the thrush is treated she will regain her enthusiasm.

Mothers often are concerned that any milk expressed while they have nipple thrush or a bacterial nipple infection might be contaminated. However, there is no evidence that a mother who has breast or nipple pain from what is considered a bacterial or yeast infection needs to discard her stored expressed breastmilk.[11]

White Spot

Features of a white spot

A white spot (also known as a milk blister, bleb or blocked nipple pore), about the size of a pinhead, may appear on the nipple when an opening to a milk duct becomes blocked. This condition is commonly associated with a blocked duct or mastitis (either as a precursor or successor). A white spot can cause nipple pain during breastfeeds.

Treatment for a white spot

A white spot needs to be removed. Sometimes continuing to breastfeed may be all that is required for a white spot to burst and for the milk to release from the duct behind it. Other times, soaking the nipple in warm water (e.g. by leaning over a bowl of warm water) for 10 minutes or so, followed by gentle rub over the white spot (e.g. with a clean towel and a bit of olive oil), can help loosen and burst it. However, it may need to be pierced with a sterile needle by a medical adviser.[1]

Once the white spot has been burst, mothers often find a plug or thin, spaghetti-like strands of milk come out. These can be removed by gently but firmly wiping around the opening.

Skin Conditions

Skin conditions (e.g. eczema, dermatitis or psoriasis) can also appear on a mother's breast/areola/nipple.

Features of skin conditions affecting the breast/areola/nipple

- Affected area is red, itchy and sore to touch
- Skin on the affected area looks scaly or flaky
- The mother would usually have other areas of skin on her body that are affected

Treatment for skin conditions affecting the breast/areola/nipple

Management often involves avoiding using soap and nipple creams, but advice from a medical adviser should be sought.[1]

'Breastmilk Jaundice'

Jaundice is a condition where there is a build-up of bilirubin in the blood. Bilirubin comes from the breakdown of old red blood cells. It is the pigment in blood that makes a baby with jaundice look yellow.

Early *physiological* jaundice appears between days two and seven of life. It is usually physiological (meaning that it is normal and nothing to worry about) and clears spontaneously after a few days. Frequent and effective breastfeeding helps jaundice clear more quickly, so the mother should be encouraged to breastfeed her baby as frequently as possible.[1] If jaundice is severe, phototherapy (light treatment) may be needed.[2]

Prolonged jaundice describes jaundice that begins after the seventh day and continues for several weeks. It is usually caused by hormones or other substances in the mother's milk, so it is sometimes referred to as 'breastmilk jaundice'. Breastmilk jaundice is harmless and clears by itself.

Many healthy, exclusively breastfed babies are jaundiced. If such a baby has normal newborn screening tests, is growing well, feeding well, passing regular normal-coloured bowel motions, passing plentiful clear urine and is generally well, even prolonged jaundice is usually not a concern. Bilirubin is actually thought to be an antioxidant and so may protect a baby from oxygen-free radicals which can damage tissues.

If the jaundice is due to a more serious condition there are usually other signs, such as:

- High bilirubin levels which appear within the first 24 hours after birth
- Pale, infrequent bowel motions
- Abnormal newborn screening tests
- Dark urine
- Signs of infection (e.g. poor feeding, lethargy, low tone, difficulty breathing, fever)
- Enlarged liver and spleen [3]

Management in these situations involves a medical adviser investigating and treating the suspected condition, and in most cases breastfeeding can continue.[4]

SECTION F:
BREASTFEEDING
MOTHER'S DIET

Does a Breastfeeding Mother Need to Maintain the Perfect Diet?

In short, a mother does not need to maintain a perfect diet to provide quality milk for her baby. A poor diet is more likely to affect the mother than her baby.

What do I need to eat while breastfeeding?

Breastfeeding increases a mother's requirements for most nutrients. It is recommended for a breastfeeding mother's well-being that she eats generous amounts of a variety of nutrient-dense foods from all the major food groups (e.g. fruits and vegetables, whole-grain breads and cereals, calcium-rich dairy products and protein-rich foods such as meats, fish and legumes).[1] See the National Health and Medical Research Council publication *Australian Dietary Guidelines* (2013) for detailed information about healthy eating for your well-being while you are breastfeeding.

What do I need to drink while breastfeeding?

It is recommended that a breastfeeding mother drinks fluids (e.g. water, juice and milk) according to her thirst. It is not necessary to drink fluids above this level.[2]

Will what I eat/drink affect my breastmilk supply?

What, or how much, a breastfeeding mother eats and drinks is unlikely to have any significant impact on her milk supply.[3] In fact, mothers in developing countries produce as much milk as those in developed countries.[4] The main determinant of milk supply is how frequently and effectively your breasts are drained. The more frequently your breasts are effectively drained, the more milk is made.

Flavours and picky eaters

Flavours are known to pass through to a mother's breastmilk from her diet so if you wish to help your child develop a taste for fruit and vegetables, for example, make sure you eat them.[5]

Also, babies who are breastfed exclusively for 6 months may be less likely to be picky eaters in early childhood compared with babies who were introduced to complementary foods before 6 months.[6]

The book *Baby-led Weaning* (2008), by Gill Rapley and Tracey Murkett, is a valuable resource for introducing family foods (complementary/solid foods).

Iodine, Vitamins and Fats

A mother's diet is largely independent of the composition of her breastmilk. For example, the lactose and protein content of breastmilk is not affected by a mother's diet.[1] However, there are a few nutrients in a mother's diet that can affect the concentration of her milk that she should be aware of:

Iodine

A mother's diet can affect the iodine content in her breastmilk.

According to the National Health and Medical Research Council (NHMRC) Public Statement on Iodine supplementation for pregnant and breastfeeding women (2010): *"The NHMRC recommends that all women who are pregnant, breastfeeding, or considering pregnancy take an iodine supplement of 150 micrograms (μg) each day. Women with pre-existing thyroid conditions should seek advice from their medical practitioner prior to taking a supplement."*

Vitamins

There is a relationship between the content of vitamins in breastmilk and the maternal diet.[2] For most breastfeeding mothers, diet will ensure that breastmilk provides all the necessary vitamins for the baby.

However, under certain situations as described below, a breastfeeding mother may need to be aware of her vitamin B12 or vitamin D status:

Vitamin B12 – The milk of vegan (and some vegetarian) mothers is likely to be deficient in vitamin B12 so a vitamin B12 supplement may be advisable.[3]

Vitamin D – Regular sunlight exposure can help prevent vitamin D deficiency, but the safe exposure time for children is unknown. Sun Smart provides a 'vitamin D tracker' to help work out how one's UV exposure compares with recommended UV exposure for vitamin D. See www.sunsmart.com.au/vitamin-d/tracker-tool.asp. If a baby's and/ or mother's exposure to sunlight is considered inadequate, vitamin D supplements may be advisable. Breastfed babies who are particularly at risk of vitamin D deficiency are those:

- Who are dark-skinned
- Whose mother is vitamin D-deficient
- Who receive too little sunlight (e.g. by living at higher latitudes)[4]

See the kellymom website at www.kellymom.com for more information on Vitamin D and the breastfed baby.

Fats

Although the overall amount of fat eaten in a breastfeeding mother's diet does not affect the overall amount of fat in her milk, the types of fats she consumes have some effect over the types of fats in her milk.[5] So if you wish to increase the levels of long-chain polyunsaturated fatty acids (such as omega 3 fatty acids) in your breastmilk, eat more. These types of fatty acids form major constituents of brain and nerve tissue and are needed in early life for mental and visual development.[6]

Good sources of omega 3 fatty acids include:

- Oily fish, such as salmon, sardines and blue-eye travella
- Eggs and meats, such as lean beef and chicken
- Plant sources, including linseed/flaxseed, walnuts, soybeans and canola oil[7]

Are there Any Foods I Need to be Cautious About?

Fish that is high in mercury

According to the NSW Food Authority: "*The benefits of breastfeeding your baby far outweigh any risk posed by the insignificant amount of mercury that might be present in breastmilk.*" It indicates that the critical time when a mother needs to limit her mercury intake is before and while she is pregnant. In this way, "*insignificant amounts of mercury will be present in your breastmilk – not enough to affect you or your baby*".

According to the Dietitians Association of Australia, "*breastfeeding women must not consume more than the recommended [see below] amounts of fish due to the risk of consuming too much mercury*".

The recommended fish intake for breastfeeding mothers, according to the Dietitians Association of Australia, is that the following fish should be eaten no more than once a fortnight (up to 150g) with no other fish to be eaten in that fortnight:
- Shark (flake)
- Broadbill
- Marlin
- Swordfish

The following fish should be eaten no more than once a week (up to 150g) with no other fish being eaten in that week:
- Orange roughy (also sold as sea perch)
- Catfish

It is indicated that most other varieties of fish caught and sold in Australia contain low levels of mercury and can be eaten without concern. The National Heart Foundation recommends consuming two to three serves of 150g of oily fish a week for heart health.

Caffeine

The transfer of caffeine into your breastmilk varies considerably depending on how well your body absorbs and eliminates it. In general, about 1% of the caffeine you consume ends up in your milk and peak caffeine levels in your milk occur approximately 60 minutes after caffeine consumption.[1]

Young babies can be particularly sensitive to caffeine. The average elimination half-life of caffeine is 6 hours in non-smoking adults (i.e. 6 hours to get rid of half the caffeine). Newborns, on the other hand, have an average elimination half-life of caffeine of 80 hours (even more for premature babies). This means that it takes a long time for a newborn to get rid of caffeine from her body. Due to this long excretion time, it is possible for caffeine to accumulate into significant amounts in a newborn. By 5 to 6 months of age the average elimination half-life of caffeine is 2.6 hours.[2]

Anecdotally, breastfeeding mothers report that a high consumption of caffeine (e.g. more than 300mg a day) can lead to various symptoms in their baby, such as: irritability, jitters, colic, constipation and poor sleeping patterns.[3] Maternal caffeine consumption in moderation (e.g. up to 300mg a day or approximately three cups of tea/coffee) is unlikely to cause any problem for babies, but it is a good idea to be more conservative if your baby is newborn or premature. Observing your baby for any signs of her being affected by the amount of caffeine you consume is the only way to determine if the amount you are consuming is having an effect.

If you are concerned about your caffeine consumption, you could call one of the breastfeeding and drug information lines (see chapter 75).

This table may help you keep track of your caffeine consumption:

Milligrams of caffeine in a 150mL cup	
Brewed or filtered coffee	90mg
Soluble instant coffee	63mg
Decaffeinated coffee	3mg
Tea	32-42mg
Cola	16mg

Source: (Nehlig & Debry 1994) [4]

Alcohol

It is safest for breastfeeding mothers to avoid any alcohol consumption, especially within the first month after delivery.[5]

Time is the only thing that reduces the amount of alcohol in a mother's breastmilk. 'Pumping and dumping' your milk does not hasten the removal of alcohol. The amount of alcohol in a mother's milk is the same as the amount of alcohol in her blood. Alcohol does not accumulate in breastmilk; it leaves at the same rate that it leaves the blood. So when a mother's blood alcohol levels are zero, so is her breastmilk alcohol level.

Alcohol will be in a mother's breastmilk 30 to 60 minutes after she begins drinking it. It generally takes about 2 hours for an average woman's body to clear the alcohol from one standard drink, 4 hours from two standard drinks, 6 hours from three standard drinks, and so on.[6]

These guidelines may be helpful if considering consuming alcohol while breastfeeding:

- Avoid alcohol consumption for the first month after delivery
- Thereafter, limit alcohol intake to no more than two standard drinks a day
- If consuming alcohol, do so just after breastfeeding
- Consider expressing milk in advance if you wish to consume alcohol [7]

It is also suggested that you read the Australian Breastfeeding Association brochure, *Alcohol and breastfeeding: a guide for mothers* (2010). Visit www.breastfeeding.asn.au for details.

If you are concerned about alcohol consumption you can call one of the breastfeeding and drug information lines (see chapter 75).

What About Food Sensitivity?

In most cases, there are no foods that breastfeeding mothers need to avoid completely.

Substances from a breastfeeding mother's diet can enter her milk. A small percentage of breastfed babies display symptoms of a food sensitivity by reacting to something in their mother's diet through her milk. In most cases, however, a baby with a food sensitivity does not show any significant signs of it while being exclusively breastfed but rather begins to show more significant signs once she starts to eat the offending food(s).

Food sensitivity is a broad term which covers food intolerance and food allergy. Food allergy involves an overreaction of the body's immune system to a particular food (commonly a food protein). Food intolerance does not involve a reaction from the body's immune system but rather often involves stomach or bowel upsets (commonly to naturally occurring or added chemicals in food). Food intolerance is much more common than food allergy.

Overall, most food sensitivities in young children improve with time. However, food allergy may form an initial step in the 'allergic march'. The allergic march is a concept that describes how allergic conditions in infancy (eczema and food allergy) may progress to other allergic conditions (asthma and hay-fever) later in childhood.[1] Also, while most children 'outgrow' allergies to cow's milk, egg, soy and wheat, allergies to nuts are usually lifelong.[2]

Cow's milk protein allergy is one of the most common types of food allergies. The incidence of cow's milk protein allergy is lower in exclusively breastfed babies compared with artificially fed or mixed-fed babies. Only about 0.5% of exclusively breastfed babies show reproducible clinical reactions to a cow's milk protein allergy and most of these are mild to moderate. Breastfeeding should be promoted for the primary prevention of allergy, but breastfed babies with proven allergy to cow's milk protein (particularly if severe) should be treated by allergen avoidance, whereby the mother continues to breastfeed but avoids the causal foods in her diet[3] and medical advice should be sought.

It is important to note that it is not useful or effective for a mother to restrict her diet during pregnancy or breastfeeding in order to reduce the likelihood of her child developing an allergy.[4]

The list below includes some common signs that a baby with food sensitivity may display. She may show many or only a few. Please note that the presentation of a baby with a food intolerance or a food allergy can be similar, and can co-exist in some babies. (The signs with an asterix are associated with food allergy rather than food intolerance).

Signs of food sensitivity in babies[5]
- Family history of food sensitivity
- Spits up milk frequently or vomits (see chapter 38)
- Irritability
- Cries inconsolably for long periods
- Sleeps little and wakes suddenly with obvious discomfort
- Intestinal upsets such as constipation or diarrhoea
- Bowel motions that contain mucus
- Poor growth (if the sensitivity is severe)
- Eczema (if severe, more likely food allergy-associated)
- Hives
- Swelling of lips, eyes and/or face*
- Rash, often around mouth*
- Breathing difficulties, e.g. wheezing*
- Frequent runny nose and watery eyes*
- Bowel motions that are bloodstained*
- Anaphylaxis*

If you are concerned that your baby may have a food sensitivity, it is important to seek specialised individual diagnosis and management. Many major children's hospitals have allergy departments that specialise in this area. Visit the Royal Children's Hospital, Melbourne, website at www.rch.org.au and go to the department of allergy and immunology section, or the Australasian Society of Clinical Immunology and Allergy website at www.allergy.org.au, or Royal Prince Alfred Allergy Centre, Sydney, website at www.sswahs.nsw.gov.au/rpa/allergy.

What About Lactose Intolerance in Babies?

Lactose is the sugar in breastmilk and is made within the breast. Lactase is the enzyme that is required to break down lactose. Lactase is made in the tips of the tiny folds of the gut. A mother's diet (e.g. how much lactose or dairy products she consumes) has nothing to do with the amount of lactose in her milk. The lactose content of breastmilk is about the same at the start as it is at the end of a breastfeed.[1]

Broadly, there are two types of lactose intolerance in babies: congenital and secondary.[2]

Congenital lactose intolerance

Congenital lactose intolerance is an extremely rare genetic condition where a baby is born with a deficiency in the enzyme lactase. A baby with congenital lactose intolerance would fail to grow well from birth and requires a specialised lactose-free artificial milk.

Secondary lactose intolerance

Secondary lactose intolerance is the most common form of lactose intolerance in babies. It can result if the gut lining is damaged because this inhibits the lactase that is made in the tips of the tiny folds of the gut. Hence, it is important to treat the cause of the damage in order to eliminate the secondary lactose intolerance. Examples of causes of secondary lactose intolerance include:

- A food sensitivity (see chapter 36)
- A parasitic infection
- Coeliac disease
- Crohn's disease

- Bowel surgery
- Gastroenteritis[3]

Symptoms of secondary lactose intolerance in an exclusively breastfed baby are:
- Green frothy/very liquid bowel motions
- Irritability (i.e. sleeps little, cries a lot)
- Is very 'windy' (i.e. passes wind frequently)

Note that the above symptoms are also common in a baby who has lactose overload (see chapter 15). In order to differentiate between lactose overload and secondary lactose intolerance, a baby with lactose overload also typically:
- Is under 3 months
- Has a large output
- Has an average to above-average weight gain
- Has a mother with an oversupply

When the cause of the secondary lactose intolerance resolves, the gut can heal and the intolerance goes away. For example, if the cause of an exclusively breastfed baby's secondary lactose intolerance is a cow's milk protein allergy, if the mother eliminates cow's milk protein from her diet, the secondary lactose intolerance in her baby will disappear. Even if it is not picked up that a baby is lactose-intolerant, continuing to breastfeed will not harm your baby as long as she is otherwise well and growing normally. In fact, breastmilk can help the gut to heal.[4]

For these reasons, a baby with symptoms of secondary lactose intolerance should continue to be breastfed (while the cause of the secondary lactose intolerance is addressed) and not be put on to a soy-based or special lactose-free baby artificial milk.[5] These artificial milks should be recommended only if the baby is already fed artificial milk or there are concerns about her growth.

If you are concerned that your baby may have secondary lactose intolerance, speak to your local medical adviser or to a dietitian who has an interest in breastfeeding (lactation) or infant feeding (see www.daa.asn. au).

Gastro-Oesophageal Reflux (GOR) and Gastro-Oesophageal Reflux Disease (GORD) in the Breastfed Baby

In this book, gastro-oesophageal reflux (GOR) is the term used for a common, benign, physiological condition whereby contents of the stomach come back up into the oesophagus (the tube connecting your mouth to your stomach). You may have felt GOR yourself (e.g. during pregnancy, after having eaten a spicy meal, after a large icy-cold drink, or if you have burped when lying down). GOR can often be managed conservatively, without the need for medical intervention.

On the other hand, in this book gastro-oesophageal reflux disease (GORD) is the term used for a pathological condition, where GOR is merely a feature, and whereby a baby requires medical evaluation.

Gastro-oesophageal reflux (GOR)

GOR is common in normal, healthy babies. This is because a baby's digestive system is immature, making it easier for the stomach contents to come back up into the oesophagus.

If your baby is developing normally (e.g. gaining adequate weight and having adequate output – see chapters 45 and 46), has no signs of persistent breathing problems and is not experiencing any discomfort with GOR, it is probable that her GOR is more of a laundry problem than a medical one.

GOR statistics[1]

GOR usually:

- Occurs right after your baby feeds (as her stomach is fullest then), but it may also occur 1 to 2 hours after feeding
- Peaks during the first month of life (73% of babies experience GOR in their first month)
- During the first 2 months of life, 20% of babies experience GOR more than four times a day
- Gradually decreases during the fifth month (50% of babies)
- Largely disappears by 12 months of age (only 4% of babies still experience daily GOR by this stage)

Causes of GOR include:

- Some babies will experience GOR when they drink too much milk and/or drink it too quickly (e.g. when a mother has an oversupply and/or a fast milk-ejection reflex – see chapter 15)
- Food allergies (in particular to a cow's milk protein) can cause a baby to experience GOR. In up to 50% of the cases of GOR in babies younger than 1 year, there is an association with a cow's milk protein allergy. And in a high proportion of these cases GOR is actually caused by a cow's milk protein allergy.[2] For more on food sensitivity see chapter 36
- If your baby is fussy at the breast (e.g. pulling off to look around) she may swallow more air during the breastfeed and subsequently spit up more milk
- Teething: when teething, babies tend to dribble more and often swallow more saliva than usual. This can cause or increase GOR
- Some mothers notice that their baby begins to experience GOR when solids or a new food have recently been introduced
- Sometimes a breastfed baby may experience GOR when their mother starts taking a new medication
- A cold may result in your baby swallowing mucus and experiencing GOR more frequently
- Babies with GORD experience GOR (see below)

Vomiting

GOR in babies may range from effortless spitting up of milk to forceful vomiting.[3] Vomiting is a forceful expulsion of stomach contents through the mouth. Vomiting may be benign, but it can also cause complications, or may indicate a serious underlying disease (e.g. necrotising enterocolitis or pyloric stenosis).[4] So if your baby vomits, this should always be checked out by a medical adviser.

Gastro-oesophageal reflux disease (GORD)

GORD is a term that encompasses a variety of medical conditions of gastrointestinal (e.g. pyloric stenosis), infective (e.g. urinary tract or ear infection, or gastroenteritis), respiratory (e.g. asthma) or other (e.g. cow's milk protein allergy) origin.[5]

Incidence of GORD:

About one in 300 babies who have GOR actually have GORD.[6]

Main features of GORD include:

- More than five episodes of GOR each day
- Breast refusal (e.g. due to your baby associating feeding with pain, or if it hurts her to swallow)
- Episodes of apnoea (briefly stopping breathing)
- Anaemia
- Problems gaining weight
- Increased irritability
- Persistent respiratory problems such as aspiration pneumonia, chronic cough and wheezing[7]

Other features of GORD include the following (but normal healthy babies may also have these):

- Back arching (i.e. to try to lengthen her oesophagus to help relieve discomfort)
- Hiccups[8]

Treatment of GORD

If you are concerned about GORD, consult a medical adviser who can help you work out whether any further investigation or intervention (e.g. medication) is required.

Breastfeeding a baby with GORD or GOR

Breastfeeding is important for a baby with GOR or GORD.

- Exclusively breastfed babies experience fewer GOR episodes each day than partially breastfed babies[9]
- Babies who are breastfed experience GORD for a shorter time than artificially fed babies[10]
- Breastmilk (compared with artificial milk) leaves the stomach much faster.[11] This means there is less time for it to come back up into the oesophagus, and it is probably less irritating when it does come back up

Tips for breastfeeding a baby with GOR or GORD:

- If relevant, reduce oversupply and/or a fast milk-ejection reflex (see chapter 15)
- Keep your baby in more of an upright position during breastfeeds. For example, try feeding her with you in an upright position and with her facing you while she straddles the top of your thigh. You may need a footstool to bring your baby to the level of your breast
- Some babies prefer smaller feeds more frequently, but others prefer larger feeds less frequently
- Ensure good attachment to your breast to minimise air swallowing (see chapter 24)
- Allow your baby to finish one breast before you offer the other. Do not interrupt active suckling just to switch sides (see chapter 12). Switching sides too soon or too often can cause excessive spitting up. For babies who want to breastfeed very frequently, try switching sides every few hours instead of at every feed
- If your baby is refusing the breast, try feeding her as she wakes

(or is still half asleep), while you are standing and walking around or in another setting (e.g. outside), and try lots of skin-to-skin contact (especially if she is just a few months old)

- When burping your baby, handle her gently, in an upright position. Holding her in an elevated position for 20 to 30 minutes after a breastfeed may help reduce GOR [12]
- Handle your baby gently without jiggling her, especially soon after feeding. Your baby may be more comfortable when she is held upright much of the time
- As always, try to follow your baby's cues to determine what works best to ease her GOR

Other ways to minimise GOR and GORD

- Eliminate all environmental tobacco smoke exposure because this is a significant contributing factor to reflux [13]
- Some mothers find that limiting their caffeine consumption can help lessen their baby's GOR
- Many mothers find their baby's GOR is often worse when they lie flat on their back. Some parents find it helpful to raise the head end of the cot mattress by about 30 degrees by placing a wedge under it.
- Many parents have found that carrying their baby in a sling or other carrier can help. Avoid compressing your baby's tummy as this can contribute to increasing the GOR and discomfort. Dress your baby in loose clothing with her nappy done up loosely around her waist. Rolling your baby on to her side for nappy changes rather than lifting her legs towards her tummy can help make nappy changes more comfortable

What about thickened feeds?

The theory behind thickening breast (or artificial) milk is to make the feed heavier and hence make it stay down in the stomach and not rise into the oesophagus. Thickeners include commercial milk thickeners, rice cereal, 'cornflour' (which can be made from wheat or corn) or bean gum. While thickeners can reduce the number of times each day that a baby spits up milk, they do not change the number of times a baby's stomach contents rise into the oesophagus.[14] Thickeners do not 'cure' GOR or GORD and can cause other problems, such as increasing coughing after thickened feeds[15] or constipation.[16]

Less spitting up of milk is worthwhile if the spitting up is contributing to your baby not gaining sufficient weight. However, in babies who are healthy and growing well in spite of spitting up milk, thickeners are not recommended.

One problem with thickened feeds is that you cannot thicken milk that your baby drinks straight from your breast. It is also hard to thicken expressed breastmilk, as live enzymes in the milk work to quickly break down the starches that make up many thickeners.

Sometimes thickeners are mixed with water and given to the baby (e.g. with a teaspoon) before breastfeeding. Sometimes attempts have been made to increase the thickness of a baby's stomach contents by adding solids into a baby's diet.

It is important to consult a medical adviser before introducing anything that may assist with GOR/GORD (including thickeners). Considering that babies with GORD typically have associated medical problems (see above), they are more likely to need all their defences against allergies and infections. Since exclusive breastfeeding for the first 6 months (i.e. without any thickeners, etc) is important for a child's health,[17] this is a worthwhile aim whenever medically possible.

SECTION G:
BUT NOT EVERY
WOMAN CAN
BREASTFEED, RIGHT?

Most women can breastfeed. There are very few absolute contraindications to breastfeeding.

According to the the National Health and Medical Research Council publication *Infant Feeding Guidelines* (2012), medical reasons that preclude breastfeeding include the following.

Baby Conditions which Preclude Breastfeeding

Babies with the following conditions should not receive breastmilk or any other milk apart from a specialised artificial one:

- Galactosemia
- Maple syrup urine disease
- Phenylketonuria (some breastfeeding with this condition is possible under careful medical monitoring)

These are rare conditions and would be picked up promptly by health professionals who are caring for you and your baby, usually through newborn screening tests.

Maternal Conditions which Preclude Breastfeeding

A mother is advised not to breastfeed if she has:

- HIV. In Australia, the current national recommendation is for HIV positive women to not breastfeed. For more information on breastfeeding and HIV see the World Health Organization publication *Guidelines on HIV and Infant Feeding* (2010)
- Herpes simplex virus type 1, or syphilis, if the mother has lesions on her breast. In this case, direct contact between the lesions on the mother's breasts and the baby's mouth should be avoided until all lesions have resolved
- Breast cancer detected during pregnancy if the mother is on chemotherapy. If a mother is not undergoing chemotherapy, the breastfeeding continuation should be evaluated on an individual basis
- Untreated brucellosis. Once treatment has been completed, breastfeeding can resume
- Active tuberculosis. Due to the risk of respiratory transmission, any close contact with the baby is not permitted until the mother has finished 2 weeks of treatment. The mother can express and provide her expressed breastmilk to her baby. However, if she has an active breast lesion or tuberculosis mastitis, she can provide her expressed breastmilk to her baby only once the lesion has healed or the tuberculosis mastitis has resolved

If you are unsure or have any questions about your medical history, consult your medical adviser.

Maternal Medications and Breastfeeding

Most medications are safe to use by breastfeeding women[1] but there are some maternal medications that justify avoiding breastfeeding. These include:

- Sedating psychotherapeutic drugs, anti-epileptic drugs and opioids and their combinations may cause side effects such as drowsiness and respiratory depression and are better avoided if a safer alternative is available
- Radioactive iodine-131 is better avoided given that safer alternatives are available – a mother can resume breastfeeding about two months after receiving this substance
- Excessive use of topical iodine or iodophors (e.g. povidone-iodine), especially on open wounds or mucous membranes, can result in thyroid suppression or electrolyte abnormalities in the breastfed baby
- Cytotoxic chemotherapy requires that a mother stops breastfeeding during therapy

If you are unsure about any of the medications you are taking, consult your medical adviser and call one of the breastfeeding and drug information lines (see chapter 75).

SECTION H:
LOW MILK SUPPLY

It is widely regarded that the vast majority of women are capable of producing more than enough milk for their babies. Two major keys to achieving this are obtaining adequate support and accurate information. We know that in the early weeks post-partum, prolactin receptors are formed in the glandular tissue of the breast. The more prolactin receptors that are formed in the early weeks (in response to frequent feeding) the better the milk-producing capacity later (i.e. more milk early means more milk later). Many women struggle with a perceived low milk supply (i.e. they think there is a problem when there actually is not). If your baby is showing indications of receiving adequate breastmilk (see section I) your supply is adequate. If you do have a low milk supply, there are strategies you can undertake to increase it (see chapter 44).

Primary Low Milk Supply

When primary low milk supply is the problem, most mothers are able to at least partially breastfeed, and there are steps that can be taken to maximise milk production (see chapter 44). If a mother is concerned that she may struggle with her supply, seeking advice from an International Board Certified Lactation Consultant before her baby is born can be very helpful (see chapter 75). A galactagogue (a substance that helps to boost milk supply) may be suggested. Some of the reasons for a primary low milk supply problem include:

Insufficient glandular tissue/hypoplastic breasts

Some women's breasts do not develop normally so they may not make enough milk-producing glandular tissue to meet their baby's needs.[1] Causes may be genetic or may be linked with hormonal conditions (e.g. polycystic ovarian syndrome), especially if the onset was pre-pubertal. It is possible that environmental contaminants may contribute by binding in place of regular hormones to hormone receptors, altering normal hormonal function.[2] Glandular tissue grows during each pregnancy and breastfeeding stimulates the growth of more, so this may be less of a problem with subsequent babies.

Hormonal or endocrine problems

There are other conditions where hormones play a role which may also contribute to low milk production because making milk relies on hormonal signals being sent to the breasts. Examples are polycystic ovarian syndrome,[3] thyroid problems,[4] obesity,[5] diabetes,[6] severe bleeding after giving birth,[7] placental problems (e.g. retained placenta[8]) and hormonal problems associated with a difficulty in conceiving.[9]

Previous breast surgery

Some women who have had breast reduction or enhancement surgery find that they have a problem with milk supply.[10] Nipple piercings can also be considered a type of breast surgery because it may damage milk ducts.[11]

How much these surgeries affect breastfeeding varies widely, depending on how the procedure was done, how much time has passed between the surgery and the birth of the baby, and whether there were any complications that might have caused scarring or damage.

Some women who have had previous breast surgery may be able to exclusively breastfeed without any difficulty. Others may be able to partially breastfeed.

Using hormonal birth control

There are many forms of hormonal birth control. For example, there are hormonal birth control pills, patches, implants or injections. There are 'combination' hormonal birth control options which are both oestrogen- and progesterone-based, while other hormonal birth control options are progesterone-only-based.

Many breastfeeding mothers who use hormonal birth control find that their milk production does not change (particularly when their hormonal birth control is progesterone-only based). Other breastfeeding mothers notice a drop in their milk supply with hormonal birth control (particularly with 'combined' options).[12]

In the early weeks after birth, there is more potential for hormonal birth control to affect milk supply because a woman's body at this time is more sensitive to progesterone and oestrogen. Gradually a mother's body can become less sensitive and there is less potential for a mother's milk supply to be affected by hormonal birth control.[13] It is generally recommended that progesterone-only-based options for hormonal birth control not begin during the first 6 weeks after birth, and oestrogen-based (or combined) options not begin during the first 6 months.[14]

If you are concerned about how the use of hormonal birth control may affect your supply, contact your doctor or one of the breastfeeding and drug information lines (see chapter 75).

Taking certain medication or herbs

There are some medications which can lower milk supply. For example, pseudoephedrine (the active ingredient in Sudafed and other allergy and cold medications), bromocriptine or cabergoline (dopamine agonists) [15] or large amounts of sage, parsley or peppermint. [16] If you are concerned that a medication or herb may be affecting your milk supply, contact your doctor or one of the breastfeeding and drug information lines (see chapter 75) to discuss possible alternatives.

Secondary Low Milk Supply

Secondary low milk supply is the most common cause of low milk supply. This arises due to circumstances which have eventually led to a low milk supply, rather than there being a primary problem. When a mother has a secondary low milk supply it is usually because she did not receive good advice, support and encouragement.

Secondary low milk supply can be prevented with the right advice, support and encouragement. Even if there is an established secondary low milk supply, mothers are often able to rectify the situation and fully breastfeed when given the appropriate advice and support.

Some of the common circumstances that can lead to a secondary low milk supply include:

Supplementation

Unfortunately, the use of artificial milk is often the first 'solution' offered by some health professionals, family or friends for a range of different concerns (e.g. fussy/unsettled behaviour or wakefulness in a baby, low milk supply (which is often perceived) in a mother). Starting artificial milk supplements can either worsen a low milk supply or cause it because:

- A baby who receives artificial milk will fill up somewhat on artificial milk and not take as much breastmilk. This then tricks your breasts into producing less milk. When your baby is given artificial milk supplements, she naturally drinks less at the breast, and the breasts respond by making less milk (see chapter 10 under 'Supply equals need' and 'Does my breastfed baby need any water?')
- A baby receiving supplements from a bottle may develop a flow preference and nipple confusion (see below) which can potentially lead to her refusing to breastfeed. See chapter 60 about how to pace bottle feeds

Not feeding at night

There are many books and programs that offer sleep-training methods to get babies to sleep longer at night without waking for feeds. It is hard to resist the lure of more sleep, but for many mothers those night feeds are essential to maintain a good milk supply. Night feeds can form an important part of maintaining milk supply and ensuring that a baby receives the breastmilk she needs for optimal growth and development.

Mothers vary immensely in the amount of milk they are able to store in their breasts between feeds (see chapter 10 under 'Storage capacity'). Mothers who are unable to store large amounts of milk in their breasts generally require more frequent breastfeeds to maintain their supply.[1] So breastfeeds at night can be important. The key message here, once again, is to feed your baby according to her need because this helps ensure that your milk supply matches her needs. All this is consistent with the fact that milk production works best when the baby is fed according to her need, provided she is removing milk effectively (see chapter 10 under 'Supply equals need').

Scheduling feedings and/or using a dummy between feedings

Your breasts make milk continuously, but the rate at which milk is made depends on how well drained they are and how often they are drained. You make more milk when your breasts are well drained (contain less milk) compared with when they are not well drained (fuller). And you make more milk when your breasts are more frequently drained compared with when they are less frequently drained.

When your baby is feeding infrequently (e.g. because you have put her on a three- or four-hour schedule or because you are giving her a dummy to stretch out the time between feeds), your breasts are less well drained (fuller) for longer periods. This results in milk production slowing. When babies are breastfed in response to their cues, they tend to feed more frequently. This means the breasts are more drained more of the time and continue to produce plenty of milk.

Using a dummy may also contribute to nipple confusion (see below).

Jaundice

Jaundice (see chapter 32), for example, can make your baby sleepier than usual, so she does not wake to feed as often as she would otherwise.[2] In such situations, it may be necessary to wake her for breastfeeds (see chapter 48). It is important to be guided by your midwife, child health nurse or an International Board Certified Lactation Consultant in these situations (see chapter 75).

Birthing practices

Practices undertaken around the birth (e.g. caesarean section, epidural anaesthesia, narcotic medication, intravenous fluids) can sometimes affect a baby's ability to attach to the breast and feed effectively.[3]

Although not always possible, birthing naturally using non-medicinal options for pain relief (e.g. a TENS machine, hypnotherapy, water, massage, heat packs or focused breathing) can help to ensure a mother and baby are optimally geared for breastfeeding straight after the birth.

While it may be necessary for certain birthing practices to occur, it is helpful to be aware of their potential effects so that strategies can be implemented to keep their effects to a minimum, and so that breastfeeding can be initiated as soon as possible after birth. Skin-to-skin contact between you and your baby as soon as possible after birth is one of the best things you can do to facilitate breastfeeding (see chapter 16).

It is also a good idea to get an International Board Certified Lactation Consultant (IBCLC) to thoroughly assess your baby's initial breastfeeds to help ensure that she is breastfeeding effectively (i.e. attaching well, stimulating your milk-ejection reflex, sucking nutritively and showing signs of receiving adequate milk – see chapters 24, 11, 12 and, 45 and 46 respectively). Some hospitals employ IBCLCs (check with your hospital), or you may need to obtain a private IBCLC (see chapter 75). If it is deemed that your baby is not breastfeeding effectively, various strategies may be suggested. With time, patience, plenty of skin-to-skin contact and baby-led attachment (see chapters 16 and 17 respectively) your baby will eventually attach and breastfeed well.[4]

Sucking difficulties (e.g. due to tongue tie)

Sometimes babies have mouth abnormalities (e.g. tongue tie, high palate or cleft lip/palate) or a neurological condition which makes it difficult for them to get the milk from your breasts.

Tongue tie means the thin membrane of tissue at the base of a baby's mouth is holding her tongue too tightly, so she cannot use it properly to extract milk. When breastfeeding, a baby extracts the milk by lowering her tongue to create a vacuum.[5] A baby can usually do this well, as the membrane at the base of the tongue is pliable enough to enable her to lower her tongue to create the vacuum. But for some babies with a tongue tie, the membrane is tighter and/or shorter which restricts the movement of her tongue and can make it more difficult for her to extract the milk.

Breastfeeding mothers who have a baby with tongue tie often have ongoing problems with nipple trauma because their baby is unable to attach optimally to the breast.

If your baby has a tongue tie, it is often picked up in hospital. However, if it has not been picked up and you are concerned – particularly if you notice that she is unable to stick her tongue out over her lower gum or cannot elevate her tongue towards the roof of her mouth – you can specifically request that she be assessed for a tongue tie (e.g. by a midwife in hospital or your child health nurse when discharged from hospital). You can then obtain a referral to see a paediatrician. If your baby is diagnosed with a tongue tie that is causing problems, the tight membrane can be clipped and your baby's ability to breastfeed will improve quickly. It is helpful to consult an International Board Certified Lactation Consultant who can help a baby to relearn to breastfeed with her 'new' tongue. See www.tonguetieclipit.com for more information.

If you suspect your baby is not feeding well, check with an International Board Certified Lactation Consultant (see chapter 75) or a speech pathologist with the relevant skills and experience.

Nipple confusion

Nipple confusion can occur when a baby has to cope with different sucking techniques (e.g. when feeding from a bottle versus the breast).

The way in which a baby feeds from the breast is very different from the way in which she feeds from a bottle. When drinking milk from the breast, a baby takes a much more active role. She must open her mouth wide to attach to her mother's breast, and take the nipple far back into her mouth. In fact, for optimal attachment (and to prevent nipple trauma) a mother's nipple needs to be drawn right back in her baby's mouth to reach the junction between her baby's hard and soft palates. This means that a good amount of breast tissue will be in the baby's mouth. The tongue is forward and down, under the nipple and breast, cupping the breast and extending over the baby's bottom gum and lip. The baby moves her tongue to its lowest position to create a vacuum to extract the milk. The baby performs a combination of nutritive and non-nutritive sucking to extract the milk or not respectively (see chapter 12). This active participation when breastfeeding means she is in control of how much or little milk she receives. This is why it is very difficult for an exclusively breastfed baby to be overfed (see chapter 15).

When a baby drinks milk from a bottle, the teat is typically only a short distance inside her mouth so she does not have to open her mouth wide. Also, when she drinks from a bottle her tongue is curled up and back in her mouth. A baby feeding from a bottle takes a considerably more passive role. A firm bottle teat in a baby's mouth provides a strong stimulus for a baby to suck and the fast flow of milk means she must continue to suck or else be flooded with milk. It is possible for a baby to take milk from a bottle even when she is not hungry/thirsty and it is impossible to know for sure if the caregiver-derived amount of milk in the bottle is exactly what the baby needs.

Some mothers notice that when their baby has to feed from both the breast and the bottle, it makes breastfeeding more difficult. For example, some mothers find that:
- Their baby has more difficulty attaching to the breast
- Their baby becomes generally fussier at the breast, and in some cases will refuse to breastfeed
- They suffer increased nipple trauma with breastfeeds as the baby somewhat 'unlearns' how to breastfeed most effectively

If you find any of the above happening, it is very likely you will be able to get breastfeeding going well again for you and your baby. Call the Australian Breastfeeding Association National Breastfeeding Helpline, or seek advice from an International Board Certified Lactation Consultant (see chapter 75). Also see chapter 60 about how to pace bottle feeds.

Flow preference

A baby who gets a continuous fast flow of milk from a bottle with little active participation may soon develop a preference for this over the active participation needed to extract a slower flow from the breast. The only question is how quickly this flow preference can occur. Some mothers have reported that it can happen after only one or two bottles.

See chapter 60 about how to pace bottle feeds.

Unnecessary weaning or expressing

Sometimes a mother will be told that she needs to wean, or express and dump her breastmilk, when she really does not need to (e.g. while she is taking a certain medication). See chapter 75 for the contact numbers which provide the most up-to-date information on the use of drugs and breastfeeding.

Expressing is different from a baby feeding at the breast in terms of milk extraction and hence the stimulation of milk supply. No matter how sophisticated the pump is, or how skilled mothers are at expressing, nothing compares with what a baby drinking well at the breast can do.

Maternal illness or menstrual cycle

Some mothers report a drop in milk supply after a bout of mastitis or at different points in their menstrual cycle (e.g. around ovulation). This may be due to temporary biochemical changes that occur within the milk-producing cells of the breast during a bout of mastitis or around ovulation.[6]

As well, some mothers report a drop in milk supply after any type of febrile illness.

For most mothers who experience these, a few days of more frequent feeding is often all that is required to increase their supply. If a mother finds that she needs more help, sometimes a galactagogue can help (see chapter 44). Speak to your medical adviser or International Board Certified Lactation Consultant (see chapter 75).

Increasing Breastmilk Supply

For specific individualised assistance whenever you have a concern about your milk supply, it is advisable to call the Australian Breastfeeding Association's National Breastfeeding Helpline or consult an International Board Certified Lactation Consultant (see chapter 75).

There are various ways to increase breastmilk supply. Often, the first thing is to ensure that your baby is correctly positioned and attached and is drinking effectively (see chapters 24 and 12 respectively). This will help ensure that milk is being adequately removed from your breast. And since breastmilk production works on a supply-equals-need basis (see chapter 10 under 'Supply equals need'), the more milk removed from your breasts, the more milk your breasts will make.

The next thing to do is to keep your breasts well drained as frequently as possible. This is because the more drained (less full) a breast is, the faster the rate that milk is produced. This can be achieved by:

- Offering your baby more feeds (e.g. a 'top-up' feed perhaps an hour or so after the last feed has ended)
- Waking your baby for more feeds (e.g. before you go to bed or whenever you hear your baby stir at night)
- Switch feeding, which entails offering her each breast for a second time straight after she has drunk from both breasts.
- Offering the breast as a way to settle your baby rather than other settling methods

If your baby is reluctant to take extra feeds, expressing between feeds can help (see Part 3). Again, this will keep the breasts as well drained as possible to ensure milk production is kept at a high rate.

Also, when trying to boost your milk supply, spending as much time skin-to-skin with your baby can help. This is because skin-to-skin contact helps boost the levels of hormones involved in producing milk.

Mothers who still struggle with low milk supply despite more frequent feeding may find it helpful to speak to a medical adviser about using a galactagogue. A galactagogue is a substance that helps to boost milk supply by increasing prolactin levels. In order to gain the most benefit from using a galactagogue, it is important for milk to be removed effectively and frequently from your breasts.

The book *The Breastfeeding Mothers Guide to Making More Milk* (2009), by Diana West and Lisa Marasco (both International Board Certified Lactation Consultants), is a valuable resource for identifying causes of low milk supply and establishing how to increase it.

SECTION I: INDICATORS OF ADEQUATE BREASTMILK INTAKE

Many parents worry about whether their baby is getting enough breastmilk because they cannot see how much they are getting. Fortunately there are ways in which you can tell whether your baby is getting enough.

Early Indicators of Adequate Breastmilk Intake

The bowel motions of a baby who is receiving adequate amounts of breastmilk will go through a series of predictable changes early on.[1] Her first bowel motion will be black and tarry (meconium), then will change to greenish and sticky, and finally will be yellow and runny (often with small curds). The first yellow bowel motion typically appears on day four (range 3 to 15). The more breastfeeds a baby has, the sooner she will be likely to transition to yellow bowel motions and have faster weight gains.[2] In terms of frequency, a baby who is receiving adequate breastmilk will, by at least day three, have at least three bowel motions in a 24-hour period.[3]

Later Indicators of Adequate Breastmilk Intake

A breastfed baby who is receiving adequate amounts of milk will:

- For about the first 4 to 6 weeks have many yellow runny bowel motions (often with small curds) every 24 hours. After the first 4 to 6 weeks, the frequency of bowel motions in a healthy breastfed baby varies considerably; some continue to have many bowel motions each day, while others have one bowel motion every 1 to 10 days.[1] As long as the bowel motion is soft and there is a large amount and the baby is otherwise thriving and content, that pattern is not unusual
- Have urine that is clear or pale yellow[2]
- Be growing in weight, length and head circumference (see section J for more detail)
- Be meeting developmental milestones (as guided by your baby's medical adviser)

Poor Indicators of Breastmilk Intake

How much milk a mother can or cannot express is a poor measure of how much milk she has. Babies are much better at extracting milk from your breasts than a pump, and expressing is a skill that needs practice. Even with practice there are some mothers who have a plentiful supply but who find expressing difficult. This is often because they find it difficult to stimulate their milk-ejection reflex (see chapter 11) when expressing.

Another poor indicator of how much milk your baby is getting is whether she will take a bottle after a breastfeed. Many babies will, not because they are still hungry but because when a bottle teat is inserted into their mouth their instinct is to suck, and when they suck from a bottle they have no choice but to drink (see chapter 43 under 'Nipple confusion'. Also see chapter 60 about how to pace bottle feeds).

Another poor measure of how much milk your baby is getting is 'test weighing'. Babies drink varying amounts of breastmilk at each feed and so test weighing after just one feed will not accurately indicate whether your baby is getting enough milk overall. Test weighing is accurate only for measuring how much milk a baby is getting in a 24-hour period if it is performed after every feed in a 24-hour period on accurately calibrated scales by someone experienced in test weighing techniques.

Do I Need to Wake My Baby for Feeds?

Most healthy, thriving babies will wake on their own for feeds. A healthy and thriving baby will show the indicators of receiving adequate breastmilk (see chapters 45 and 46). In these cases, it is not necessary to wake a baby for feeds; you can let her run the show and feed her when she wants to be fed.

It is important to remember that crying is a late feeding cue (see chapter 1). A baby will settle into a feed much better when earlier feeding cues are picked up.

Sometimes a baby may display early to intermediate feeding cues only when rousing from sleep and may not cry; she may even fall asleep again. If this happens you may miss an opportunity to feed her. Being aware of this can help you to be on the lookout for earlier feeding cues. By having your baby sleep in your room at night you will find that you are naturally very responsive to her noises (e.g. including her squeaky noises) and will rouse easily to attend to and feed your baby.

Babies under about 6 weeks typically feed every 2 to 3 hours, with one longer stretch in between feeds (up to about 5 hours) and one or two periods where they cluster feed (e.g. feed every 1 to 2 hours). Time between feeds is counted from when the last feed began (see chapter 14).

It is normal for babies after the first post-natal breastfeed to alternate between light and deep sleep from 2 to 20 hours after birth. Then, between 20 and 24 hours, babies typically alternate between being asleep and awake, and typically cluster feed (i.e. have frequent short breastfeeds). This period of cluster feeding is typically followed by 4 to 5 hours' sleep.[1]

If your baby continues to be sleepy past the initial sleepy period and continues to not rouse easily (e.g. due to a medical condition such as jaundice or an infection, or if the baby is still affected by pain medications used during the birth), you may need to wake her for breastfeeds until she 'finds her feet' and begins to rouse more frequently on her own. It is often suggested that in these situations a baby be woken at least every three hours during the day and every five hours through the night for breastfeeds. It is important to be guided by your midwife or an International Board Certified Lactation Consultant (see chapter 75).

The following strategies may help rouse a sleepy baby and encourage her to breastfeed:

- Unwrap her, talk to her, and gently stroke her body
- Change her nappy
- A warm bath
- Insert your clean finger in her mouth to encourage sucking
- Stroke her lip and cheek
- Skin-to-skin contact, especially with the mother in a semi-reclined position
- Express a small amount of your breastmilk/colostrum and give it to her on a teaspoon or syringe, for example (see chapter 59), to give her a 'taste'

Once your baby is feeding, these strategies can also help to keep her awake and feeding well:

- Switch feeding: straight after your baby has drunk from both breasts, offer her each breast a second time
- Breast compressions: squeeze your breast to increase the flow to encourage your baby to suck nutritively and hence get more milk (see chapter 13).

Please note that babies can breastfeed even when not fully awake.

If your baby still does not breastfeed well despite all efforts, you can express and provide her with your milk/colostrum using an alternative method (see Part 3 for information on expressing and chapter 59 for alternative feeding methods). Consulting your midwife or an International Board Certified Lactation Consultant (see chapter 75) is important in these situations too.

SECTION J: BREASTFED BABIES AND WEIGHT GAINS

World Health Organization (WHO) Growth Charts

The WHO charts were developed based on a breastfed population, and it is recommended to use them to monitor breastfed and non-breastfed babies, and children from birth to 5 years, because they describe the growth of babies and children with no economic, health or environmental limits. These charts reflect the optimal and therefore portray a rate of growth that can serve as a goal for all healthy babies and children, regardless of ethnicity, socio-economic status and type of feeding.

General Guidelines for Growth in the First Year

- A baby loses up to 10% of birthweight in the first week and regains this by 2 weeks.[1] However, some studies indicate that maternal fluids during labour may artificially elevate a baby's birthweight. This suggests that a greater percentage of the initial loss may be normal in some cases[2]
- After the initial loss, a baby starts to regain weight between days four and six[3]
- Birthweight doubles in the first 6 months[4]
- By 12 months, a baby's weight is about 2.5 times her birthweight,[5] her length is about 1.5 times her birth length and her head circumference increases by about 7.6cm[6]

These are general guidelines. Please check with you medical adviser for a thorough assessment if you are concerned about your baby's growth.

Breastfed Babies Put on Weight Differently from Artificially Fed Babies

It is normal for a breastfed baby's weight gains to vary from week to week. Some weeks she may put on a small amount of weight; other weeks she may put on a large amount. It is more informative to look at a breastfed baby's weight gain over a period of 4 weeks rather than weekly to find an average weekly weight gain.[1]

In the first few months, artificially fed babies tend to grow more slowly than breastfed babies. Thereafter, artificially fed babies tend to grow more rapidly than breastfed babies.[2]

In terms of average weekly gains for a breastfed baby, there are wide individual variations. As a rough guide, the National Health and Medical Research Council recommends the following for weight gain in infancy:

- Birth to 3 months: 150g to 200g a week
- 3 to 6 months: 100g to 150g a week
- 6 to 12 months: 70g to 90g a week [3]

If there is a concern about a baby's weight gain, it is important to assess each baby individually taking into account:

- Genetic factors (e.g. weight/height of parents/siblings. If a mother and father are tall and slim, it is unlikely that their baby will end up short and plump)
- Feeding practices (e.g. is the baby feeding effectively (see section B)? Is she being fed according to need or to a schedule? The latter can potentially reduce how well a baby gains weight)
- What the baby looks like (e.g. does she have even skin colour and good muscle tone? Does she look like she 'fits' her skin?)
- Whether the baby is meeting developmental milestones. A baby

who is doing this is less likely to be undernourished
- Baby's output (see chapters 45 and 46). A baby with a good output is less likely to be undernourished
- Length and head circumference measurements (see chapter 52)
- How/when previous weight measurements were taken (e.g. were they taken soon after a breastfeed, resulting in a larger measurement, or soon after a large bowel motion, resulting in a smaller measurement? Were they taken by the same person on the same set of scales? If not, it is more likely for discrepancies to exist)

Does a Baby Need to 'Stick' to a Percentile Line?

It is common for changes (including shifts in percentiles) in growth to occur in the first 2 years. Few babies keep to the percentile line they were born on – most cross percentile lines for weight and length. One study showed that only 12% stayed on the same weight percentile on which they were born, 60% showed an upward crossing and 28% showed a downward crossing.[1]

A baby's weight at birth relates more to conditions inside the womb and maternal health rather than genetic considerations. After birth, babies gradually move to their genetically pre-programmed size and can take from 6 months to 2 years to do this. After 2 years they then follow this line, more or less, though still with some variations.[2]

All three measures – weight, length and weight-for-length – provide important information to assess growth. These may indicate if the child is growing and gaining weight, and whether the weight gain is too little, too much or just right for the length of the child.[3]

Medical investigation is required if it is noticed that a child's growth is sharply heading towards crossing two major percentile lines, or if a child's growth is above the 90th percentile or below the 10th percentile, or crosses these percentiles.[4]

Any sharp incline or decline in a child's growth line represents a very significant change in growth, and a flat growth line indicates that a child is not growing. In these situations medical investigation is also required.[5]

PART 3

Expressing

Do I Need to Express?

There are many books these days that advocate expressing. It seems expressing is the 'in thing' so expectant parents often have questions about it. Here are some things to think about when deciding whether or not you need to express.

Switching between bottle and breast

Some mothers find that their babies switch between bottle and breast seemingly without any problems, while others find this contributes to:

- Painful nipples, because the baby is 'unlearning' somewhat about how attach to the breast and feed most effectively
- Breast refusal, because the baby develops a flow preference to the faster, more continuous, flow from a bottle. (See chapter 60 for tips about how to pace bottle feeds.)

Bonding time for the father?

Sometimes it is thought that the father can have bonding time with a baby by giving her expressed breastmilk. However, fathers can bond in many other ways that are also very important. For example, they can help with things such as baby massage, bathing, settling, play time and nappy changes.

Also, sometimes it is thought that expressing means the father can do the night feeds which will help the mother get more sleep. However, experience shows that mothers still wake when their baby wakes, and often have to express at that time anyway to stop their supply dropping or simply because their breasts are uncomfortably full. So the amount of sleep a mother gets ends up being negligible compared with breastfeeding and then getting back to sleep.

Dreamfeed

Another reason why some mothers choose to express is to provide their baby with a top-up of expressed breastmilk (e.g. for a 'dreamfeed'). The dreamfeed is given just before a mother goes to bed in the hope that it may make the baby sleep for a longer stretch. This may work for some mothers but others find that the effort involved to produce the expressed breastmilk is not worth the possible result. Some mothers discover that the dreamfeed does not make their baby sleep any longer afterwards, or that it results in their baby having more wind pain. Some mothers simply decide to go to bed earlier to maximise their precious sleep time.

Other mothers may be concerned about the possibility of a dreamfeed interrupting the baby's natural sleep rhythms, or that it may create a habit, resulting in the baby expecting the same thing every night and self-waking at the same time each night for the dreamfeed. If the dreamfeed was not introduced, her baby may have gradually slept for a longer stretch anyway.

Routine

Some books advise mothers to express to help establish a routine. While there may be a few babies who fit easily into a routine, the reality for most parents with newborns is that they often are unpredictable, sleep irregular lengths and feed at irregular times. This makes more sense when we explore more about a baby's sleep and about the development of her circadian rhythm (see chapter 63).

Time factor

Many mothers soon discover that the time it takes to express is more exhausting than simply breastfeeding. With frequent feeds, numerous nappy changes (young breastfed babies tend to have many bowel motions), spitting up milk (at least 50% of babies do this), accidents at nappy changes where they get sprayed with number ones or twos or it goes over the floor or walls, settling, unsettled periods (see chapter 72), burping, and self-care (eating, showering, dressing), and all the rest, there is very little time left to express.

Even if they have the best intentions to express at points throughout the day, what if the baby is hungry and wants to feed when they had planned to express? Or what if the baby did not sleep as long or even settled to sleep when they had planned to express? Suddenly expressing seems too hard, so many mothers give up and resort to being content that this difficult period is not going to last forever (even though it can seem so at times). Many babies start to become accustomed to their environment and are generally more settled around the 3-month mark.

Sore breasts

For a sleep-deprived parent, it may seem very appealing to have a long stretch of sleep. Many fathers think that if they were to give their baby a bottle some time during the night it would allow the mother to have more sleep. However, many mothers, especially in the early weeks, find that if their baby does not wake them, soreness and fullness in their breasts when their baby has a longer sleep does. So suddenly, when there is an opportunity for a longer sleep, the mother cannot because it feels as though her breasts are going to explode and she ends up wishing for her baby to wake to relieve the discomfort.

Supply

Frequent feeding in the early weeks (which includes night feeds) leads to enhanced milk-producing capacity later (see chapter 10).

Even after the early weeks, night feeds can form an important part of maintaining milk supply and ensuring that a baby receives the breastmilk she needs for optimal growth and development. Mothers vary immensely in the amount of milk they are able to store in their breasts between breastfeeds (see chapter 10 under 'Storage capacity'). Mothers who are unable to store large amounts between feeds generally require more frequent breastfeeds to maintain their supply. So breastfeeds at night can be important to maintain milk supply. All this is consistent with the fact that milk production works best when the baby is fed according to her need, provided she is removing milk effectively (see chapter 10 under 'Supply equals need').

Reasons for Expressing

There are some more practical or therapeutic reasons for expressing, such
as:

- Your baby is unable to suck well (e.g. premature or has a
  neurological condition or has a tongue tie or cleft palate)
- You and/or your baby are in hospital and you cannot be together
  for every feed
- You have returned to the paid work force, study or other
  commitments. See www.breastfeedingfriendly.com.au for
  information about a breastfeeding-friendly workplace
- You are leaving your baby with a babysitter
- Your breasts sometimes feel too full and uncomfortable
- Your baby is refusing to breastfeed. For more information on
  breast refusal call the Australian Breastfeeding Association
  National Breastfeeding Helpline, or consult an International
  Board Certified Lactation Consultant (see chapter 75).
- To give your nipples a break if they are painful because of
  problems with attachment. Whenever you have painful nipples
  seek prompt advice by calling the Australian Breastfeeding
  Association's National Breastfeeding Helpline, or by consulting
  an International Board Certified Lactation Consultant (see
  chapter 75).

When to Express?

If a mother is breastfeeding but needs to express to store milk for later use (e.g. because she is going to be leaving her baby with a babysitter), she may find that expressing in the morning is easier. This is because breasts generally produce a greater volume of milk in the morning compared with the end of the day. Also, there is a greater tendency for feeds to be more spread out in the mornings compared with the end of the day (hence more opportunities may arise when you can express). Some mothers express between feeds while others express a small amount from a breast just before feeding.

If a mother is expressing full time, or near full time, (e.g. because her baby is premature and unable to breastfeed effectively) she will need to express at regular intervals around the clock to mimic what her baby would be doing if breastfeeding.

When expressing, following the tips to help stimulate your milk-ejection reflex can be helpful (see chapter 11). Nonetheless, for some mothers expressing is all but impossible because the milk-ejection reflex is a very conditioned response, and they find it very difficult to stimulate it with a pump. And if you cannot stimulate your milk-ejection reflex barely any milk will flow because breastmilk is not stored in the milk ducts.

Which Pump is Right for Me?

There are many factors involved in pump selection, such as:
- Cost
- Availability
- Access to electricity
- Anticipated frequency and duration of expressing
- Time constraints
- Comfort

In general, for occasional use (i.e. once a day or less), manual pumps (e.g. Medela Harmony) or personal electric pumps (e.g. Medela Swing) may suit. For frequent use (e.g. more than once a day) a personal single electric pump (e.g. Medela Swing) or personal double electric pump (e.g. Medela Freestyle or Ameda Purely Yours) may suit. When the use is very frequent (e.g. when using a pump to establish a milk supply or to maintain a full or near-full milk supply) a hospital-grade hire pump (e.g. Medela Symphony or Ameda Platinum) would generally be the pump of choice. A hospital-grade hire pump can be used for single or double pumping (most mothers use it for double pumping).

Hospital-grade hire pump (Medela Symphony)

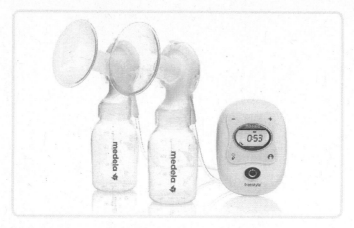

Personal double electric pump (Medela Freestyle)

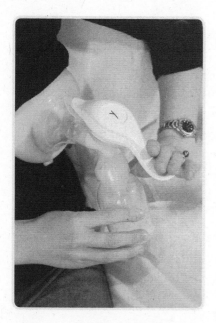

Manual pump (Medela Harmony)

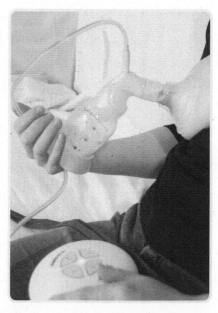

Personal single electric pump
(Medela Swing)

Breast pumps can be bought from Mothers Direct (see www.mothersdirect.com.au for more information). Details of how to hire a hospital-grade hire pump can be obtained by calling the Australian Breastfeeding Association's National Breastfeeding Helpline (see chapter 75).

Hand Expressing

Hand expressing is another option that was available long before breast pumps existed. (See video.about.com/breastfeeding/Hand-Expression-Technique.htm to see a mother hand expressing).

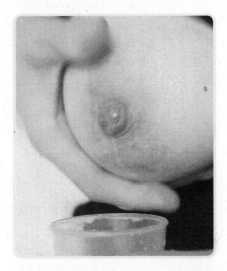

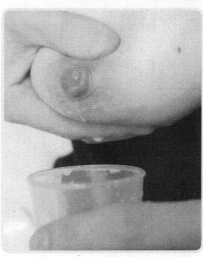

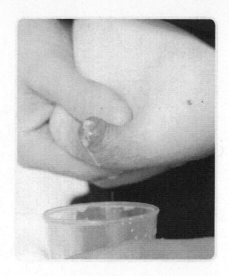

Hand expressing

Hand expressing is relatively easy to learn and may be sufficient for short-term or occasional expressing – although some mothers may also use it as a longer-term method of expressing if necessary.

Many mothers prefer hand expressing if they need to express in the first few days after the birth. This is because colostrum is produced only in small amounts and is thicker than mature breastmilk. So if expressing colostrum with a breast pump, much of it adheres to the inner workings of the pump, which makes less of it available to the baby.

Many mothers find that some hand expressing after using a pump can help remove more of the available milk from their breasts. Combining hand expressing with electric pumping has also been found to increase milk production in mothers of premature babies.[1]

How Much Breastmilk is Enough for One Expressed Breastmilk Feed?

The only precise way to know if a baby is getting exactly the right amount of milk is to breastfeed her according to her need, provided she removes milk effectively (see chapter 10 under 'Supply equals need'). In this way, the baby is in control. If she receives one expressed breastmilk feed in 24 hours it is not imperative to provide her with a precise amount. This is because when she is breastfed according to her need for the other feeds, she will even things out by breastfeeding more or less frequently, or for a longer or shorter time, depending on her need. And in this way she will ensure that she receives her required amount over 24 hours.

Nonetheless, there may be circumstances in which a baby is unable to feed from the breast (e.g. because a mother has to go out without her baby) so she will need to express. In such a situation, below are some average figures to help figure things out.

In the early post-partum period, there is a rapid increase in volume consumed by an exclusively breastfed baby. The following table displays average amounts of breastmilk consumed by an exclusively breastfed baby between 1 and 5 days post-partum. Please note that wide variations exist between individuals. The figures in this table are based on results from two studies: Neville et al (1988) and Saint et al (1984).[1]

Baby's age	Average volume consumed in 24 hours (Neville et al 1998)	Average number of feeds (Saint et al 1984)
Day 1	44mL (range -31-115mL)*	3 to 8 breastfeeds
Day 2	182mL (range 96-268mL)	
Day 3	371mL (range 218-524mL)	5 to 10 breastfeeds (days 2 to 5)
Day 4	451mL (range 275-627mL)	
Day 5	498mL (range 369-627mL)	

*Negative values are due to insensible weight loss (e.g. a bowel motion)

After the initial rapid increase in breastmilk consumption in the early post-partum period, consumption levels out. There is wide variation for when this levelling-out occurs but typically it is somewhere between days 5 and 28.

The volume of breastmilk consumed when this levelling-out occurs varies from baby to baby. What research tells us, however, is that for an exclusively breastfed baby between the ages of 1 and 6 months, the average volume consumed in 24 hours is 788mL (range being 478mL to 1356mL).[2]

Therefore, for example purposes, if a baby between the ages of 1 and 6 months was having 10 breastfeeds in 24 hours, this would equate to approximately 80mL each feed (i.e. 788mL divided by 10 feeds = 78.8mL a feed). So 80mL of expressed milk would be sufficient for this baby for one feed.

Many mothers cannot express the amount of milk 'required' for one feed in one expressing session so they express small amounts in a few sessions over a few days.

Alternative Feeding Methods

A bottle is often the first thing that comes to mind when considering feeding a baby with expressed milk. However, depending on the condition of the baby and individual mother-baby circumstances, there are alternatives. When using a bottle it can help to use pacing techniques (see chapter 60).

Alternative feeding methods include:

Cup feeding

This may seem quite foreign when hearing it for the first time, but even premature babies can drink milk from a cup. When she does, the baby takes an active role. Also, her tongue position and sucking motion mimics breastfeeding.

Cup feeding

It can take a little practice for cup feeding to be fast and efficient. For a full-term baby, cup feeding can be useful:

- When a baby is temporarily separated from her mother
- When the mother has cracked nipples which need time to heal
- For some babies with relatively minor clefts of lip and palate

For a young baby (under about 4 months) a small cup, such as a medicine cup, works best. For an older baby (4 to 6 months) you can try different cups to see what works best: a regular cup (try different sizes), a sippy cup, a no-spill sippy cup, a cup with straw (or with a built-in straw) or a sports bottle are options.

Cup-feeding method

1. Use a small cup (e.g. a medicine cup or shot glass) for a young baby.
2. Cup feed your baby only when she is fully awake and alert.
3. Wrap your baby to restrain her hands so that she cannot swipe at the cup.
4. Sit your baby upright on your lap, with her head supported, while you have one hand behind her shoulders and neck.
5. Place the edge of the cup gently on your baby's lower lip.
6. Bring the milk to the baby's lower lip. Once your baby brings her tongue forwards and realises that there is milk, she can lap the milk up. Do not pour the milk into your baby's mouth as this puts the baby in danger of aspirating the milk (having the milk 'go down the wrong way' into her lungs).
7. Maintain the level of the milk as best you can so that your baby can continually lap it up.
8. Do not take the cup away when the baby pauses, unless she pulls away. Follow your baby's cues, and allow her to resume when she is ready. Let her set her own pace.

For more information on how to cup feed, see www.nbci.ca and watch the 'Cup Feeding' video by going to the 'Information & Videos' section and scrolling down to 'Video Clips – English.'

Breastfeeding supplementer

A breastfeeding supplementer is a device that enables a baby to receive extra milk while feeding at the breast. Fine tubing carries expressed breastmilk (or artificial milk) from a container to the nipple. When the baby sucks at the breast, milk is drawn through the tubing into her mouth, along with any milk from the breast. By continuing to feed at the breast, the baby is able to control her milk intake, and nipple confusion (see chapter 43 under 'Nipple confusion') can be avoided.

A breastfeeding supplementer may be useful for a baby who has a weak suck or tires easily but is able to maintain suction at the breast. It can also be useful for a mother to provide her baby with extra milk if she has a low supply, while at the same time being able to keep the baby feeding from her breasts.

See www.breastfeeding.asn.au and www.medelabreastfeedingus.com and search the site for 'supplemental nursing system' (Medela's version of a breastfeeding supplementer). If you are considering using a breastfeeding supplementer, consult an International Board Certified Lactation Consultant (see chapter 75).

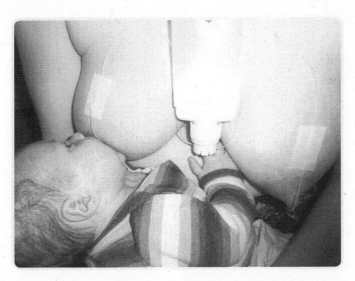

Supplemental Nursing System (Medela)

Other feeding methods:
- Spoon
- Finger-feeding

For more information on these see chapter 75 and search on the 'helpful breastfeeding websites'.

If your baby has started solids, you can:
- Mix the solids with breastmilk
- Make a breastmilk iceblock on a stick

Pacing Bottle Feeds

How a baby drinks milk from the breast is very different from how she drinks milk from a bottle (see chapter 43 under 'Nipple confusion' and 'Flow preference'). Pacing bottle feeds helps the baby to be more in control of the amount of milk she gets. This can help minimise any concerns you may have about bottle feeding interfering with breastfeeding.

How to pace bottle feeds

- Use the slowest-flow teat possible. Generally, slower-flow teats will have fewer holes, be longer, have a wide base and be made of firmer material
- Feed the baby when she is showing feeding cues (see chapter 1) rather than according to set times
- Hold the baby in more of an upright position (with her head and neck supported, as required, with your hand)
- Encourage the baby to open her mouth wide by gently brushing the teat along her lips. Once she has opened her mouth wide, place the teat in her mouth so that she ends up having a good mouthful of teat (just like she would have a good mouthful of breast when breastfeeding)
- Tip the bottle up just far enough to allow the milk to fill the teat. As milk is removed from the bottle, you will need to gradually tip the bottle up more so that the milk continues to fill the teat
- Every few minutes, tip the bottle back so that the milk no longer fills the teat to let the baby have a break from drinking (just as she would when breastfeeding)
- Stop the feed when the baby hints at being full (e.g. falls asleep, releases the teat, relaxes her hands and fingers). She may not need to drink all the milk

Just One Bottle of Artificial Milk Won't Hurt, Right?

There are very few reasons for which breastfeeding is contraindicated and a specialised artificial milk is medically necessary (see section G). Indeed, other individual circumstances may present in which careful consideration by a medical adviser or an International Board Certified Lactation Consultant may indicate the need for supplementation with donor breastmilk or artificial milk.

Apart from the above, there may be situations which you encounter when giving your baby 'just one bottle' of artificial milk may seem appealing or is suggested by a well-meaning friend, family member or even a health professional. When considering that it is important to be aware of the potential risks and weigh them up with the presenting circumstances.

Bacteria in the gut is a major determinant of one's overall health and well-being. The gut contains a large percentage of all the body's immune cells.[1]

For at least the first few months of life, a baby's gut is most susceptible to potentially harmful bacteria. This is because a young baby's gut is 'leaky' – whereby unwanted substances are more likely to 'leak' through the folds in the gut, rendering it more susceptible to damage and/or disease.[2]

There are many reasons why breastfeeding helps a baby ward off potentially harmful pathogens. For example, healthy bacteria predominate, and the pH is lower, in the gut of an exclusively breastfed baby. Also, breastmilk contains a multitude of anti-infective properties that help protect a baby from potentially harmful pathogens in her environment.[3]

However, when any artificial milk is given to a breastfed baby, especially in the first week of life, the number of potentially harmful bacteria in the gut increases (while the number of healthy bacteria decreases) and the pH of the gut rises. All this creates an environment where there is an increased risk of infection, and the baby's gut may be unable to reach its full healthy potential.[4]

Because of a baby's leaky gut, early exposure to artificial milk may increase the risk for the acquisition of the following:

- Necrotising enterocolitis (an acute inflammatory condition of the gut. Premature babies are most at risk of this condition)[5]
- Inflammatory bowel disease (e.g. Crohn's disease, ulcerative colitis)[6]
- Cow's milk protein allergy[7]
- Type 1 diabetes[8]

If breastmilk was again given exclusively, it would take 2 to 4 weeks for the gut environment to return to a state favouring healthy bacteria.[9]

Storage of Expressed Breastmilk

The following information has been adapted from The Academy of Breastfeeding Medicine Protocol Committee, *ABM Clinical Protocol #8: Human Milk Storage Information for Home Use for Full-Term Infants* (2010).[1]

Breastmilk can be stored in plastic or glass. There has been concern about possible contamination if it is stored in plastic food storage bags because of the risk of contamination if the plastic is punctured. So if you use plastic bags they should be sturdy, well-sealed and stored in an area where damage to the bag is minimised. Plastic containers made with bisphenol A (BPA) should be avoided because of the possibility of it adversely affecting the body's endocrine system. If you are unsure whether the plastic contains BPA, contact the manufacturer.

Preparation for expressing

Items used for expressing, collecting and storing breastmilk do not need to be sterilised beforehand. They just need to be washed in hot soapy water and rinsed well or washed in a dishwasher. If soap is not available, then boiling water is preferable.

The procedure is as follows:

1. Wash your hands thoroughly with warm soap and water, or a waterless hand cleanser. Dry your hands with something clean (e.g. new paper towel or clean, unused towel).
2. Separate all item parts.
3. Rinse all parts in cold water to remove residual milk.
4. Wash all parts thoroughly with hot soapy water. A brush kept just for this purpose is recommended.
5. Rinse all parts at least twice in hot water.
6. Let all parts drip-dry upside down on a clean paper towel.
7. Ensure all parts are dry before use/storage. If any drips of water

remain, dry them with a clean paper towel.

8. Use or store parts in a clean, covered container until next use.

For a healthy baby, if you are expressing several times each day you can rinse all the parts well with cold water to remove the milk, and then place them in a clean, closed container. Or you can store the items, unrinsed, in a clean, closed container in the refrigerator. All parts should be thoroughly cleaned at least once every 24 hours while the breast pump is in frequent use, or after each use if the breast pump is being used only occasionally.

Storage of breastmilk for home use

As breastmilk is continually changing to meet a baby's needs, and because freezing and/or storing it alters some of its nutritional properties, the fresher it is the better it is. Freezing breastmilk leaves its nutrient value essentially unchanged, but the immunological properties (e.g. white blood cells and antibodies) are reduced.[2] Nonetheless, frozen breastmilk is still unequivocally better than artificial milk.

Breastmilk	Maximum recommended storage duration		
	Room temperature (16–29°C)	Refrigerator (≤4°C)	Freezer (<-17°C)
Freshly expressed	3 to 4 hours	3 to 5 days	6 to 12 months
Previously frozen, thawed in refrigerator but not warmed	3 hours	24 hours	If not used, discard. Do not refreeze
Previously frozen, thawed and warmed	For completion of feed (e.g. between 1 and 2 hours)	If not used, discard. Do not re-refrigerate	If not used, discard. Do not refreeze
Baby has begun feeding	For completion of feed (e.g. between 1 and 2 hours)	If not used, discard. Do not re-refrigerate	If not used, discard. Do not refreeze

Your baby may drink the breastmilk cool, at room temperature, or warmed. Babies may demonstrate a preference.

Newly expressed breastmilk can be added to previously expressed breastmilk, provided the previously expressed breastmilk has been stored safely (see table above). It is best to cool the newly expressed breastmilk before adding it to the previously stored breastmilk to prevent the already stored breastmilk being rewarmed.

Breastmilk can be defrosted either in the refrigerator overnight, by running under warm water or by sitting it in a container of warm water. It is difficult to control the temperature when defrosting human milk in a microwave, which can cause the milk to heat unevenly. Microwaving also significantly decreases the anti-infective quality of breastmilk, which reduces its overall health properties. For these reasons, it is not recommended to defrost expressed breastmilk in a microwave.

Some mothers report that their stored breastmilk has an altered smell and taste. This is caused by the activity of the enzyme lipase (this naturally exists in breastmilk) which breaks down fat into fatty acids. This helps the baby digest the breastmilk and is not harmful, although some babies may refuse to drink it. Naturally, breastmilk that appears stringy, foul or purulent should not be fed to the baby.

There is no evidence that a mother who has breast or nipple pain from what is considered a bacterial or yeast infection needs to discard her stored expressed breastmilk.

PART 4

Sleep

In this section you will learn about, and develop an appreciation for, baby sleep and behaviour. You will learn how to work with your baby towards achieving someone who anticipates sleep times, who loves sleep and for whom sleep time is not stressful but is something you both look forward to.

There are various ways to bring up a child. No matter what anyone says, if your way works for you and your family then it is the right way for you.

Circadian Rhythms and Promoting Healthy Sleep Habits

Developing healthy sleeping habits is worth striving for. In the long term, healthy sleep habits, along with healthy eating habits and exercise, form important parts of our well-being. There is evidence suggesting that healthy sleeping habits which develop in childhood are carried through to later life.[1]

Evidence also exists that there is a link between childhood sleep problems and:

- Depression in adolescent years [2]
- Anxiety and attention problems in adolescence [3]
- Alcohol-related problems in adolescence [4]
- Obesity later in life [5]

Studies also indicate that quality sleep enhances memory and learning in children and adolescents.[6]

Circadian rhythms are our internal body clocks which help to regulate our mood, energy levels and sleep patterns. They depend on environmental cues (daylight and darkness) and social cues (e.g. bedtime rituals) to help us wake up and feel energetic during the day and enable us to fall asleep easily at night.

Circadian rhythms are governed by certain hormones, in particular melatonin and cortisol. Cortisol levels are highest when we wake in the morning and help us to get going for the day. Melatonin levels increase during the day and peak in the evening to help our bodies enter hibernation mode so we can drift off to sleep. Morning light helps regulate these hormone levels by signalling to our body clock that it needs to begin its active cycle. As the daylight fades, melatonin levels increase and we start thinking about withdrawing and going to sleep.

One does not have to be a sleep expert to know that the most powerful influences over sleep are light and darkness. Through aeons people have woken to morning light and fallen asleep in evening darkness. This cycle seems natural; we feel energetic in daylight, and yawn and become lethargic at night. When we miss out on signals, such as bright morning light or evening darkness, our circadian rhythm may shift, and as a result our bodies produce hormones at the wrong time, or stop producing the right amounts.

Understanding how circadian rhythms regulate sleep and activity helps us prevent circadian rhythm problems (and therefore sleep problems) from occurring. Developing healthy, lifelong circadian rhythms requires lifelong vigilance. Those with long-standing body-clock problems require strong light signals (such as light therapy) and need to maintain a regimen for several months or years to help reprogram their circadian rhythms. Since circadian rhythms begin to emerge when babies are about 2 months old,[7] we can help them develop healthy sleep habits from the beginning. From this age onwards, environmental cues (daylight and darkness) and social cues (e.g. bedtime rituals) can greatly influence a baby's circadian rhythm, and hence her sleep/wake patterns.

Even before a baby's circadian rhythm begins to emerge, a parent has a great influence over the sleep/awake state. For example, if a baby is drowsy and a parent provides her with something that stimulates her senses, this may make her more alert. On the other hand, if a drowsy baby's senses are not stimulated she may go to sleep.

This chapter explores points which help develop a baby's circadian rhythm and help promote healthy sleep habits from an early age.

Bedtime rituals

A bedtime ritual at night is important to help a baby get her body ready for sleep because it provides a strong social cue to help influence her circadian rhythm.[8] A bedtime ritual also helps a baby feel more comfortable and secure, as she learns to anticipate what is going to happen next. And it provides clear signals that it is almost time to go to sleep. The important thing is that the same things are done consistently, in a loving and unhurried manner, before putting your baby down for a sleep.

Bedtime ritual before night-time sleep begins

Before your baby goes to sleep at the beginning of the night, the following (in chronological order) may form part of a bedtime ritual:

- A warm bath
- Baby massage (see below)
- 'Wind-down time' (e.g. singing some calming songs or reading books when the baby is older) and dimming the lights
- Take your baby to her sleeping room
- Put her sleep attire on (e.g. sleeping bag – see chapter 65)
- Say a special goodnight phrase as you put her down in her sleeping place*.

A breastfeed may, especially for a young baby, form part of a bedtime ritual too.

*Sleeping place. This refers to wherever a parent chooses to place the baby for sleep (e.g. cot/ bassinet). No matter the place, it is up to the parent to ensure the sleeping place is safe. For more information see the SIDS and Kids website at www.sidsandkids.org.

Daytime bedtime ritual

It is helpful to implement a bedtime ritual before daytime naps too. The bath and massage parts can be left for the more elaborate night-time bedtime ritual. A bedtime ritual before day naps may just include (in chronological order):

- Wind-down time
- Take your baby to her sleeping room
- Put her sleep attire on
- Say a special goodnight phrase as you put her into her sleeping place

A breastfeed may, especially for a young baby, form part of a bedtime ritual before daytime naps too.

Look out for tired cues

A young baby (under about 4 months) is ready to be prepared for sleep during the day when she starts to show tired cues (see chapter 2). It is very helpful to begin wind-down time as soon as a young baby begins to show tired cues. Remember that when a baby reaches the crying stage of being tired, she is probably getting overtired which makes it more difficult for her to settle. A young baby (under about 6 weeks) may reach the crying stage within minutes, so keep wind-down time very brief. Then, as soon as you see your baby's first yawn, begin to put her sleep attire on, say your special goodnight phrase and put her down for a sleep. This can help to make the road to dreamland smoother.

In terms of the night-time bedtime ritual, the bath and massage can happen before your baby begins to show tired cues. This usually fits in nicely, because as a baby approaches 3 months her longest stretch of awake time is typically in the late afternoon/early evening so you have more time here to implement the night-time bedtime ritual.

As a baby gets older, tired cues become less relevant. From about 6 months, there is more scope for a baby to be able to stay awake contentedly without getting overtired. From 3 months, day naps can occur at certain times to help establish a baby's sleep/wake pattern and her circadian rhythm. Examples of how a baby's naps can be structured are indicated in chapter 69 under 'Daytime naps'.

Below are guidelines on how long a baby can typically stay awake in total in between day naps (when the baby has slept well in the sleep prior). This is helpful to have an estimate of when to be on the lookout for tired cues.

- 0 to 6 weeks, 1 hour
- 6 weeks to 3 months, 1.5 hours
- 3 to 4 months, 1.5 to 2 hours
- 4 to 6 months, 2 to 2.5 hours
- 6 to 9 months, 2.5 to 3 hours
- 9 to 12 months, 3 to 4 hours

Bedtime rituals for the first 2 weeks or so

It is helpful to establish bedtime rituals as early as possible. For the first few weeks, however, it is common for a baby to doze off after/during a breastfeed. So, during these early weeks, it is often not possible for a baby to have more awake time after a feed to then enable a complete bedtime ritual. (Indeed, young babies do not have to be bathed every day.) There are certain aspects of a bedtime ritual that can be implemented from the beginning however, including:

- Take your baby to her sleeping room
- Put her sleep attire on
- Say a special goodnight phrase as you put her down in her sleeping place

Bedtime rituals after about 2 weeks

Other aspects of a bedtime ritual (e.g. wind-down time) can begin to be implemented more consistently as your baby begins to be able to have more awake time after daytime breastfeeds.

By the time your baby is 2 months old, the complete night-time and daytime bedtime ritual can be done consistently.

Length of time spent on a bedtime ritual

The length of time spent on a bedtime ritual may be gradually lengthened as a baby gets older and is able to contentedly stay awake longer. For the first month or so, it is important to keep any wind-down time brief (e.g. a few minutes) to help avoid your baby getting overtired, making it more difficult for her to go off to sleep. Putting your baby to sleep as soon as you see the first yawn can help make the road to dreamland much smoother.

Routine bedtime and wake-up time

Waking up and going to bed close to the same time help reinforce a consistent sleep rhythm and remind your brain when to release, and when not to release, sleep and wake hormones. Routine bedtimes and wake-up times also help develop daily structure (see chapter 69 for more detail on daily structure).

Routine bedtime

It helps to be consistent about your baby's bedtime at night. A routine bedtime between 6pm and 8pm works well for many parents. This is because it:

- Accounts for an 11- to 12-hour sleep overnight (even if interrupted with breastfeeds until they sleep this length of time uninterrupted – see chapter 64)
- Means starting the day at a reasonable hour of the morning (i.e. between 6am and 8am), especially for when your child begins school. This is a long way off, yes, but healthy circadian rhythms take a lifetime of vigilance, as described earlier in this chapter
- Allows parents time in the evening to unwind without children around

After the routine bedtime, all breastfeeds are treated as night feeds. This means that light and noise levels are kept low, and no wind-down or play time occurs (see chapter 70 for more detail).

Routine wake-up time

Starting each day with your baby around the same time (e.g. following on from above, between 6am and 8am) also helps to develop your baby's circadian rhythm. Starting the day means treating every feed after the wake-up time as a day feed (i.e. feed in the lighter part of the house) and including 'play' times after feeds and bedtime rituals, as age appropriate.

With a young baby (under about 3 months) we cannot control their wake-up time and bedtime to perfection; they are merely things to aim for. Young babies often sleep at irregular intervals around the clock, have short awake periods and unsettled periods (see chapter 72). However, with persistence, the dividends will pay off.

Breastfeeding and circadian rhythms

Breastmilk contains tryptophan, an amino acid that is used by the body to manufacture melatonin. Tryptophan levels rise and fall according to maternal circadian rhythms, so it is possible for breastfeeding to help develop a baby's circadian rhythm.[9] Thus a mother's circadian rhythm and fluctuating sleep/wake hormone levels, which have been well-established for years, help develop her baby's circadian rhythm.

Baby massage

There is evidence to suggest that a baby who is massaged in the evening (e.g. after a bath) sleeps better at night by increasing levels of the (sleepy) hormone melatonin.[10] Also, as part of a bedtime ritual, massage provides a baby with an environmental signal that it is almost time for sleep,[11] which can help her go to sleep and help the quality of her sleep.

Baby massage involves touching your baby using long, firm, but gentle and smooth strokes. A natural oil (e.g. olive) works well. For more information (including classes) see infantmassage.org.au. There are also some good videos on baby (infant) massage on www.youtube.com.

Daylight during the day and darkness at night

As mentioned above, circadian rhythms use light and dark signals to tell your body when to produce wake or sleep hormones. Bright light during the day, such as sunshine, helps your body wake up in the morning and start the day with vigour. Likewise, dark signals in the evening help your body get ready for sleep. So it is important to expose your baby to light during the day and darkness at night (see chapter 70) to help her sleep better.[12]

Sleeping environment

Keeping your baby's sleeping environment quiet, boring and as dark as possible for sleep times and night feeds is important to help promote sleep. However, it is also important for a parent to go about things normally during the day, even when the baby is sleeping. After all, your baby has been used to all these noises in the womb and needs to continue to be accustomed to everyday noises throughout the day. In terms of darkness during the day, having the blinds closed is sufficient.

Also, if your baby remains in the same sleeping place for any given sleep period without being interrupted or transferred from one sleeping place to another, she is more likely to sleep for a longer stretch, obtain the benefits of the different types of sleep (see chapter 68) and to be more content in general.

Calm and positive approach

Remaining calm and relaxed is not always easy when caring for a young baby. However, babies can pick up when we are feeling stressed. Likewise, when we are stressed we are less likely to pick up on what our baby is telling us. For both reasons our baby will be less likely to fall asleep easily when we are stressed.

Life with a new baby can be stressful, exhilarating, exhausting, rewarding, challenging, exciting, daunting, etc. Having, and accepting, as much support, encouragement and assistance as possible is paramount in order to keep as calm and positive as possible. Many mothers will tell you that they can be at home alone, exhausted and overwhelmed with an unsettled baby, but when a refreshed father comes home and takes the baby, she settles immediately.

Awake times

Keeping your baby awake, as age appropriate, after daytime feeds for some 'play' helps her body promote more restful sleep at night (i.e. increases her sleep drive) which replenishes her body and consolidates new brain connections. It is very important for your baby to not be over-stimulated with awake time during the day, however, because this can lead to overtiredness. Be on the lookout for your baby's tired cues.

'Play' time for a young baby does not have to be anything elaborate. Everything is new to them. Simply lie your baby in various safe places to experience different sounds, smells, visions and sensations. Babies love different shades of light/dark (e.g. sunshine through blinds), faces (especially your face), outside, and the sound of your voice.

Below are guidelines on when it is likely that a baby will be able to stay awake for some 'play' after a feed that has been given soon after she wakes.

- 0 to 2 weeks – rarely (common for a baby to fall quickly to sleep after a feed)
- 2 to 4 weeks – very occasionally
- 4 to 6 weeks – sometimes
- 6 to 8 weeks – frequently
- 8 weeks onwards – consistently

Avoid substances that promote sleeplessness

Some of the things that we eat or drink can have sleep inhibitors in them (e.g. caffeine and some medications), and it is possible for these substances to cause your baby to be more wakeful (through your breastmilk). If you are taking any necessary medication that you feel may interrupt your (or your baby's) sleep, talk to your doctor about an alternative. See chapter 35 for more information about caffeine.

Daytime naps – sleep promotes sleep

A baby who goes to sleep at night tired, and has received her quota of sleep during the day, is more likely to sleep better at night. If a baby goes to bed overtired and has not slept well during the day, she is much less likely to sleep well. In this way, sleep promotes sleep in a baby.

Is She Sleeping Through?

Concerns about your baby's sleep

It is common for mothers to worry if their babies are not sleeping through the night by a certain age. After all, everyone knows they are 'supposed to', and you will hear stories from family and friends about their child sleeping through at 6 weeks, 3 months or 6 months etc. Even when the mother has no problems with her baby waking at night, she still worries that this is a problem because everyone seems to ask about it. It seems everyone's baby is doing this except yours. In many ways, sleeping through can be perceived as a status thing that a mother needs to live up to.

What is sleeping through?

There are, in fact, many interpretations of what 'sleeping through' actually is. For some, for example, sleeping through is 5 hours of uninterrupted sleep, and for others it is 11 to 12 hours. As many mothers have experienced, babies can continue to feed during the night from 6 weeks of age to 2 years, or even longer. This is normal and nothing to be concerned about.

In this book, sleeping through is defined as 11 to 12 hours of uninterrupted sleep. Most children are eventually able to sleep this long, uninterrupted, at night; it is just a question of when.

When will my baby sleep through the night?

Sleeping through is something that will occur in time when your baby is developmentally ready, even if you do nothing about it. Getting your baby to sleep through the night is not a battle to be won, as it is so often portrayed in books and the media. It is a developmental milestone that different babies will reach at different times. At some point your child will sleep through the night (usually somewhere within the first 2 years) even if you do nothing to encourage it. Many mothers find that by taking a more relaxed approach, and trusting that it will come in time, they can feel better about the whole experience. You will be able to rest peacefully in your heart and mind knowing that your baby reached this in her own time when she felt secure enough to do so.

It is common for breastfed babies to not sleep through the night for a long time. On the other hand, some breastfed babies start sleeping through when a few months old. If you and your baby enjoy night-time feedings, why not continue? It is a great way to spend time together, particularly if you are apart during the day. Most importantly, do not be concerned if your baby is not sleeping through the night when others' babies are.

Even if a baby happens to sleep through the night from an early age many parents find she begins to wake through the night again after a while. This is because there are many reasons why a child will wake at night (see below).

This book gives you a great head start into understanding your baby's sleep and behaviour, and to helping develop healthy sleep habits from the beginning. However, down the track, if you find it a problem when your older baby or toddler wakes at night, the parenting educator and author Elizabeth Pantley has written helpful books on this topic.

Reasons why a baby wakes at night

Many health professionals tend to look at a baby waking at night from a nutritional standpoint, but this is only part of the story. Babies wake for many reasons, not just for nutrition. Many mothers will tell you that there are other reasons. These include:

- Hunger – babies have a small stomach capacity and breastmilk is easily digested
- Thirst
- Need to suck
- Discomfort (e.g. nappy rash)
- Lonely, fearful
- Noise, or lack of noise

- Illness (e.g. ear infection, respiratory infection, urinary tract infection, common cold)
- Events during the day may affect your baby's sleep. For example, she may wake and want comfort from her mother to compensate for being separated during the day
- Separation anxiety. When your baby is about 6 months old, her brain starts to mature in ways that greatly enrich her emotional life. She begins to be aware of her own feelings, and she begins to form a strong emotional attachment to her primary caregiver. This may explain why many babies who were previously sleeping longer stretches at night may begin to wake more frequently. Once your baby starts forming strong attachments she is more likely to feel separation anxiety. She is also more likely to anticipate your departures and protest. And she is more likely to become upset if she wakes and you are not there
- Mastering new motor skills. When babies are learning to crawl, walk or accomplish other milestone feats, the excitement associated with this and all the new connections that are being made in their brains may interfere with their sleep (see chapter 74). During such periods, babies may be more resistant to going to sleep at night and/or wake at night more often because of the heightened level of brain stimulation
- Teething. Many mothers report that their babies wake more frequently in the days or weeks before a new tooth erupts
- Room temperature. Some babies will wake if they get too hot or too cold
- Introduction of solids. Some babies wake up more frequently at night around the time solid food is introduced. This may be because they are experiencing unusual sensations in their digestive systems
- Night terror
- Nightmare

Emotional needs are every bit as real as your baby's physical ones, and having them met is crucial to your baby's overall development. After the first few months your baby will begin to associate the breast with far more than just a way to satisfy hunger and thirst. It becomes a place of comfort, security, warmth, closeness and familiarity. The act of breastfeeding is not just nourishing; it is nurturing.

Sleep associations

A sleep association is something that one associates with going to sleep. For aeons, breastfeeding has been (and still is) the most natural way for a baby to fall asleep. In many ways, breastfeeding and a baby's sleep are intertwined. For a baby, there really is no more lovely way to fall asleep than when she is nestled close to her mother, feeling her warmth, heartbeat and breathing, and drinking her milk.

Gradually, as a baby grows and develops, breastfeeding and a baby's sleep become separate entities. How quickly or slowly this occurs is up to each mother/baby pair. Regardless of when it happens, a bedtime ritual (see chapter 63) can form an important sleep association for a baby. This is simple to implement and helps a baby become accustomed to, and anticipate, sleep time. If a bedtime ritual is consistently implemented in a loving and unhurried manner from a very early age (by the time a baby is just over 3 months old) it is more likely that a baby will consistently settle to sleep with little or no fuss. A consistent bedtime ritual also makes it more likely for a baby to resettle between sleep cycles, or during or at the end of active sleep (see chapter 67).

Breastfeeding when baby wakes in the night

When you breastfeed your baby at night, you are not teaching her a bad habit; you are teaching her that you are there for her when she needs you.

Mothers all around the world know that breastfeeding is the quickest (and most natural) way to get their baby back to sleep when they wake at night. This is because breastmilk is a natural sleep tonic. It contains a wonderful hormone called cholecystokinin (CCK). CCK induces sleepiness in both a baby and her mother.[1]

Also breastfeeding, and the skin-to-skin contact associated with it, boosts oxytocin levels in a baby and her mother. Oxytocin enhances a mother's maternal feelings and gives her a sense of calm. It also provides mother and baby with a natural sedative and overall feel-good effects.

Breastfeeding your baby when she wakes (no matter the reason) through the night will not hinder her ability to eventually sleep through the night. A bedtime ritual (see chapter 63) can help your baby gradually learn to anticipate and become accustomed to sleep times. In the meantime, a breastfeed is the fastest and most natural way to get her back to sleep.

After the first few months, one thing that you may consider doing at night, however, is to gently put your baby's sleep attire (e.g. sleeping bag – see chapter 65) back on after the breastfeed, before placing her back down to sleep. This means that the last thing that is done before she goes back to sleep is having her sleep attire put on, rather than the breastfeed itself.

Breastfeeding and length of sleep that a parent gets at night

Early months

Parents of babies who are exclusively breastfed at night during the first 3 months may sleep longer (by 40 minutes on average) than parents of babies who are given artificial milk, particularly when the baby is close to her mother.[2] This may be because:

- The hormone cholecystokinin, which promotes sleepiness, is released in mother and baby during breastfeeding
- The quality of a mother's sleep improves when breastfeeding. Mothers who breastfeed have increased slow-wave sleep, part of their deep or non-rapid-eye-movement (NREM) sleep. Slow-wave sleep is an important marker for sleep quality because those with a higher percentage of slow-wave sleep report decreased daytime fatigue [3]
- A mother does not have to prepare anything to breastfeed

Parents of babies given artificial milk may also report more sleep disturbance than parents of babies who were exclusively breastfed at night.[4]

Swaddling and Baby Sleeping Bags

Swaddling is the practice of wrapping a baby for sleep. The ideas behind swaddling are that it helps a baby feel secure by mimicking the confined environment they experienced in the womb, and it dampens the startle reflex (which produces spontaneous, jerky movements, even in sleep) which can disturb a baby's sleep. A muslin sheet (very thin type of fabric) can be used in summer, and in winter a thicker cotton material.

Please note that a baby should be swaddled only if she is sleeping on her own separate sleeping surface.

There are many methods to swaddle a baby and you will probably discover that your baby likes to be swaddled in a particular way. Many babies like to have their hands up around their chest, because this is the position they often take in the womb, and it can be comforting. Ensure that the swaddle is loose enough to not restrict your baby's breathing or movement of her hips, and allows enough room at the bottom to allow her to move her legs to help pass a bowel motion or wind while sleeping.

If you like, a cot sheet can be tucked securely at the sides and bottom of the cot to help keep the swaddle in place (or to add extra warmth). Remember that if you are ever in doubt, it is best for a baby to be too cold rather than too hot, as overheating is a risk factor for SIDS.

Some babies do not like being swaddled – they fight to get their arms free. If your baby does not like it, you could simply wrap her with her arms out and/or tuck in a sheet securely at the sides and bottom of the cot. Or you could use a baby sleeping bag instead.

By 3 months, babies have more control over their arm movements and are more accustomed to their environment. This is the time to cease swaddling (if you haven't already). In addition, around this time they will be able to roll on to their tummy, so it is imperative they are no longer swaddled so that they can use their arms to clear their face to reduce the risk of SIDS.[1]

Some babies begin to roll on to their tummy whenever they are placed on their back once they learn how to (as if they programmed to practise their new skill over and over). If your baby is over 6 months, it is usually suggested you let her remain on her tummy when sleeping if she has already rolled over. If she is under 6 months, however, it is suggested that she not be swaddled but that you use a firmly fitted sheet that is tucked into the sides and end of her cot to discourage (or prevent) her from rolling on to her tummy.

To help the transition from being swaddled to not being swaddled, you can leave one arm out for a few days and then both arms out (i.e. wrap her from under the armpits down) before stopping completely.

When your baby is no longer being swaddled, I recommend using a baby sleeping bag. From 3 months on, and particularly from 6 months on, babies move a lot in their sleep. You might put them on their back at the foot end of the cot and later find them on their tummy up the other end. Baby sleeping bags also ensure that a baby stays warm no matter how much she moves around. Many have a 'TOG' scale which can be used as a guide for which type of sleeping bag and underlying clothes are appropriate for a particular temperature. To save money, you can buy a sleeping bag that is 1 to 2 sizes bigger than your baby (just ensure that it is not so big that she can wriggle her head down into it).

Sudden Infant Death Syndrome (SIDS)

SIDS is not nearly as prevalent as it used to be. This is largely because of the SIDS and Kids Safe Sleeping health promotion campaign (see www.sidsandkids.org for more information). Since its inception in the early 1990s, the campaign has reduced the incidence of SIDS by 80%.[1]

How to sleep your baby safely:[2]

- Put her on her back from birth (not on her tummy or side)
- Ensure there is nothing that may cover her face (e.g. doonas, pillows, lambswool, bumpers or soft toys)
- Ensure a smoke-free environment (before and after birth)
- Provide a safe sleeping environment (e.g. safe mattress and bedding)
- Sleep her in her own safe sleeping environment next to the parents' bed for the first 6 to 12 months[3]
- Breastfeed! Breastfeeding helps protect against SIDS[4]

Sleep Duration

Sleep patterns vary widely between different babies. In general, a newborn baby sleeps about 14 or 15 hours in every 24. A newborn typically sleeps between 1 and 5 hours for any one sleep period, and her pattern of sleep and wakefulness is irregular. Her sleep periods are shorter and more frequent than in an older child. Often the pattern of a young baby's sleep is dictated by her need to feed.[1]

By the age of 12 months, the average length of time slept in 24 hours is 13.9 hours. As your baby matures, consolidation of sleep duration and timing is seen during the night. Babies begin to have longer awake periods during the day and daytime sleep can be organised into discrete naps.[2] By 12 months a baby is typically having 1 or 2 daytime naps of between 1 and 2 hours (see chapter 69 under 'Daytime naps').

Iglowsten, Jenni, Molinari and Largo (2003) tracked 493 Swiss children from birth to 16 years. Below is a table which displays the average sleep times of these children between 1 and 24 months. The figures can serve as a rough guide to your baby's sleep. Keep in mind, however, that this study focused on a specific group of children: Swiss children born between 1974 and 1993. Different individual circumstances and cultural factors may mean that your baby's sleep patterns differ significantly from those in this study.

Age	Average total sleep time (hours)	Average total night sleep (hours)*	Average total day sleep (hours)	50% of babies sleep between	96% of babies sleep between
1 month	14 to 15	8	6 to 7	13 and 16	9 and 19
3 months	14 to 15	10	4 to 5	13 and 16	10 and 19
6 months	14.2	11	3.4	13 and 15.5	10.4 and 18.1
9 months	13.9	11.2	2.8	12.8 and 15	10.5 and 17.4
12 months	13.9	11.7	2.4	13 and 14.8	11.4 and 16.5
18 months	13.6	11.6	2	12.7 and 14.5	11.1 and 16
24 months	13.2	11.5	1.8	12.3 and 14	10.8 and 15.6

Adapted from (Iglowsten, Jenni, Molinari & Largo, 2003).[3]

*Please note that these figures refer to the total average length of time spent asleep during the night but do not necessarily indicate that these hours of sleep are not interrupted (e.g. for a breastfeed).

Sleep Cycles

Like adults, babies sleep in cycles. One sleep cycle of an adult lasts about 90 minutes, whereas a baby's lasts about 60 minutes.[1] In adults, light sleep is referred to as REM (rapid-eye-movement) sleep and deep sleep is referred to as NREM (non-rapid-eye-movement) sleep. In a baby under 6 months, REM sleep is referred to as active sleep, and NREM sleep is referred to as quiet sleep.

A sleep cycle of a baby under 6 months is made up of approximately 40 minutes of active sleep (60%) and 20 minutes of quiet sleep (40%).[2] As your baby gets older, her sleep cycle length increases, the length of time spent in deeper, quiet sleep increases and the length of time spent in lighter, active sleep decreases. By the time a child is about 5 years old, her sleep resembles adult sleep – sleep cycles of approximately 90 minutes – and more is spent in the deeper NREM sleep (75%) versus the lighter REM (25%).[3]

Active sleep in babies may be mistaken for awake behaviour. This is because a baby in the active phase of sleep:

- May make rapid body movements and twitches (mostly fingers, toes and face muscles)
- May make many different vocalisations (even a few loud cries)
- May open her eyes
- Has an irregular breathing pattern
- Will wake easily if disturbed

It helps to be able to recognise this and give your baby a few minutes to resettle. Active sleep is important for learning and processing information.[4]

On the other hand, a baby in the quiet phase of sleep:

- Makes very little facial or body movement
- Does not vocalise
- Has a regular breathing pattern

- Is not easily roused

Quiet sleep is important for rejuvenation and growth.[5]

A baby under 3 months will usually start with an active sleep stage before going into quiet sleep. Then, after about 3 months, this is gradually reversed. She will begin to more frequently start with a quiet sleep stage before going into active sleep. By 6 months this is usually consolidated, such that there will be very few sleep cycles in which she enters active sleep first.[6]

The terminologies of quiet and active sleep are usually replaced by NREM and REM sleep respectively by 6 months. By this age, quiet sleep starts to differentiate into the four stages of the more mature form of NREM sleep, the percentage of time spent in active sleep is decreasing (especially during daytime naps) and a baby is less likely to display the characteristics of active sleep.[7] This reflects the increasing maturity of a baby's brain and central nervous system.

Sleep cycles summary

Age	Active/REM (light)	Quiet/NREM (deep)	Sleep cycle length	Sleep entered with
0 to 3 months	40 minutes (60%)	20 minutes (40%)	60 minutes	Active sleep
3 to 6 months	40 minutes (60%)	20 minutes (40%)	60 minutes	Active sleep or quiet sleep
6 months	40 minutes (60%)	20 minutes (40%)	60 minutes	NREM sleep
12 months	Gradually decreasing to adult levels	Gradually increasing to adult levels	70 minutes	NREM sleep
2 years		80 minutes	NREM sleep	
5 years	20 minutes (25%)	70 minutes (75%)	90 minutes	NREM sleep

Understanding baby sleep cycles and active sleep can help identify whether she is waking or just making 'sleeping sounds'. These may be grunts, groans, puffs or grizzles and frequently last a few minutes.

Frequently they start between 3 and 4 weeks of age. They often occur around the 40-minute mark of her sleep (i.e. at the end of active sleep before entering quiet sleep), within the first 40 minutes of her sleep (i.e. during active sleep), or between sleep cycles.

During these episodes, a baby is often close to, or even fully, asleep but may open her eyes briefly and survey her surroundings (especially if she is between sleep cycles). Familiar surroundings often result in a baby going back to sleep if left alone. However, if the surroundings are different from those when the baby went to sleep (e.g. lights were on, now off, or parent was present, then not, or the baby fell asleep in her parent's arms, then is in her cot), she may wake fully.

So whenever possible, if a baby can be put down for a sleep when drowsy, but not fully asleep, and be allowed to fall asleep in the surroundings in which she will wake, she will mostly go back to sleep if that is, in fact, what she needs.[8]

Listen and watch your baby in these situations. If she is showing feeding cues (see chapter 1) she wants to be fed.

Sometimes a baby needs only a short nap of 30 or 40 minutes. For the first 3 months, the length of each sleep period is irregular. This can make it difficult to determine if a baby needs more sleep when she starts making noises around the 40-minute mark. In this situation, you could allow her to make some noises for a few minutes to give her a chance to resettle, and if she does not then get her up for a feed. Fortunately, a baby's behaviour, sleep and feeding patterns are typically more predictable after about 3 months (see chapter 69).

In reality there will be times, especially within the first few months, when a baby wakes up fully but is still tired (i.e. does not resettle). In this instance, offering a 'top-up' breastfeed in a calm manner can often help get her back into a calm, sleepy state to be able to put her down again. Getting a baby who has not had enough sleep back to sleep quickly can help prevent a challenging situation whereby a cycle of a short feed, short sleep, short feed, short sleep, and so on, develops.

Daytime Guidelines

Providing some structure to the day helps strengthen a child's circadian rhythm and reduce the likelihood she will be irritable because she is tired. Many children thrive on consistency. It helps them feel secure as they can anticipate what is coming next and they feel like all their needs are being taken care of. When things are done consistently, with a loving yet firm approach, children are much more likely to follow along automatically. Bedtime struggles will become unusual. Children will look forward to bedtime without struggle or resistance when they have positive interactions with parents during a bedtime ritual. A bedtime ritual in an unhurried manner, with a loving, yet firm and consistent, approach fosters security and promotes the child's ability to fall asleep without protest (see chapter 63).

Processes throughout the daytime

During your baby's awake periods (between day naps), the following processes can help provide some structure to the day (in chronological order):

- Breastfeeding soon upon waking from a day nap (and at any other time that is required)
- Burping and nappy change
- 'Play' time (length varies according to your baby's age and how well she slept in the prior sleep period)
- Wind-down time once your baby starts to show tired cues (e.g. singing calming songs, or reading books when your baby is older)
- Sleep attire is put on your baby (e.g. swaddle/sleeping bag) once tired cues are becoming more pronounced (e.g. she begins to yawn)
- Special goodnight phrase is spoken

- Your baby is put in her sleeping place. Whenever possible, aim for your baby's eyes to be open when you put her down

Wind-down time needs only to be very brief (e.g. a few minutes) for the first couple of months so that she does not doze off during this time, but rather has opportunities to take herself off to sleep in her sleeping place.

It is not uncommon for a baby to need more than one breastfeed during an awake period. Many mothers notice that from about 3 months babies can be easily distracted by their environment. Often they find their babies have more than one breastfeed in an awake period (e.g. perhaps even two or three). Sometimes a baby is not interested in feeding more frequently during the day but will wake up more frequently at night to ensure she gets her 24-hour intake quota. Being aware of a baby's feeding cues will help a mother to work out when her baby needs to feed (see chapter 1).

Also from about 3 months on, many babies begin to become very efficient at drinking from a breast (sometimes a breastfeed may last only a few minutes). As long as a baby is showing indicators of receiving adequate breastmilk (see chapter 46) and her mother continues to feed her according to her need, speediness at feeding is rarely an issue.

Daytime naps

The following provides guidelines on how many day naps babies require for each of the following age groups:
- 0 to 3 months: four naps (each approximately 2 hours)
- 3 months to 12 months: three naps, gradually down to two (each approximately 1.5 to 2 hours)
- 12 months to 3 years (or more): two naps, gradually down to one (each approximately 1.5 to 2 hours)[1]

The first and second day naps can gradually begin later. For example, if a baby starts the day about 7am:
- By 3 months a baby can usually stay awake until 8.30am before going down for her first nap. She can then stay awake until about 12.30pm before going down for her second (earlier if she

had only a short first nap)
- By 9 months she could go down for her first nap about 9.30am and her second nap about 1.30pm (earlier if only short first nap)
- By 18 months she could be having just one nap each day (starting about 12.30pm)

Between 6 and 9 months a baby often does not need a third day nap. This means that she may be awake for a longer stretch in the hours just before bedtime.

Bath

Young babies do not need to be bathed every day. Of course you can bath your baby every day if you wish. Some young babies love to have a bath; others simply do not enjoy them, so a bath every second or third day is fine. Gradually, as a baby gets used to her environment, she will consistently enjoy bath time. Babies who are not fond of baths tend to be happier if they are fed before them and if a cloth is wrapped around them during the bath (to make them feel less exposed). As part of establishing a ritual before bedtime at night you may choose the early evening as the time to give your baby a bath.

Nappy-free time

Babies spend a lot of time in nappies. It is healthy for a baby's skin to have at least one nappy-free session during an awake period each day, when she can kick her legs, get some fresh air on her bottom, and perhaps even some gentle sunlight on her body (good for getting some vitamin D and for reducing mild jaundice).

Nappy changes

An exclusively breastfed baby's bowel motions are normally runny, perhaps with little seed-looking specks through them, and are a yellow/mustardy (or orange) colour. Some mothers indicate that their exclusively breastfed babies' bowel motions are greenish. This is usually nothing to worry about; sometimes it may just indicate that a mother has an oversupply of milk (call the Australian Breastfeeding Association's National Breastfeeding Helpline for more information; see chapter 75).

Breastmilk is much more easily digested and used by a baby's body compared with artificial milk. For these reasons, a breastfed baby's bowel motions are much less pungent and there is less volume.

All that is required to clean the bottom of an exclusively breastfed baby is some cotton squares and water. No baby wipes are necessary. When they begin solid food, some wipes may be necessary to help clean up a bowel motion which may become a bit messier.

Some parents smear a small amount of nappy rash prevention/ treatment cream (e.g. Sudocrem) on to a baby's bottom after cleaning as a way to help prevent nappy rash. If your baby's bottom becomes particularly red, seek advice from your child health nurse.

Supervised tummy time

Young babies spend a lot of time on their back, so unless we place them on their tummy they will not go there until they learn to roll (usually not for a few months). Two or three times each day, from as early as possible (even day one), place your baby on her tummy during her awake time (e.g. after nappy change) for a few minutes or until she gets sick of it (she will let you know). The more often you do this the more time she will happily spend on her tummy. Tummy time promotes muscle development and motor control around a baby's neck, shoulders and shoulder blades, which is important for the preparation towards crawling.

Burping

Breastfed babies take in less air than bottle-fed babies. This is because a good seal is created when a baby breastfeeds where little, if any, air can be sucked in. In some cultures the concept of burping a baby is completely foreign. Nonetheless, a short break and cuddle in between breasts or after a feed, with your baby upright over your shoulder, will often help to ensure that your baby is comfortable. Some babies will burp easily but others do not. Spending lots of time trying to 'get a burp up' can be stressful and your baby may not even need to burp.

Many mothers find that their baby can settle back to sleep after a breastfeed without being burped, especially at night.

See chapter 3 under 'Upper wind pain' for more information.

Tips for going on outings with your baby

Heading out with your baby, especially the first few times, can feel quite daunting. It can seem there is so much to think about and organise even for the most simple of outings. In time, however, heading out with your baby will become easier and you will figure out what works best for you both. At times you will have little choice about when you need to leave; other times you may be able to plan ahead to make the outing run a bit more smoothly. For these times, the following suggestions may be helpful.

For a baby under 4 months or so, it can help to leave when she is first getting tired. If you do, there will be a good chance she will fall asleep in the car and when you arrive at your destination you can transfer her to a pram to continue her sleep. At this point she might grizzle (see chapter 71) for a few minutes before going back to sleep. If she does not seem to be resettling, it can help to offer her a quick breastfeed before putting her back into her pram to resume sleep.

If you are heading out on your own (e.g. leaving the baby with your partner), it can help to leave straight after a feed to maximise the length of time before the next feed.

From about 4 months, many babies are able to stay awake for at least 2-hour stretches and be contentedly awake in a pram for longer. This makes heading out after a feed another option.

Night-Time Guidelines

Lights and noise levels low

Throughout the night, keep night feeds as low-key as possible. This means having the room as quiet and dark as possible. This will help your baby develop her circadian rhythm (see chapter 63).

Nappy changes during the night

Breastmilk is a natural sleep tonic (see chapter 64). In order to keep a baby in this calm, sleepy state after night feeds, it can help to change her nappy between sides (or before a feed if she takes only one breast), rather than after the feed. And unless she has a very wet or dirty nappy, or has nappy rash, you do not need to change her nappy at night.

Processes throughout the night

Throughout the night when your baby wakes to be fed, the following processes can help (in chronological order):
- Gently remove her sleep attire (e.g. swaddle or sleeping bag)
- Breastfeed
- Change her nappy between sides (or before feeding her if she takes only one breast, as long as this does not make her too upset before the breastfeed)
- Burp her if necessary (see chapter 69 under 'Burping')
- Gently put her sleep attire back on
- Put her back down to resume sleep

Settling Techniques

Many parents find that the most difficult thing about caring for a newborn baby is the settling to sleep part. There will be occasions when your baby will need help to go to sleep, especially during the first few months.

At various times a young baby will:
- Settle to sleep with little or no fuss
- Settle to sleep with quite a bit of fuss
- Need some help to go to sleep
- Need a lot of help to go to sleep

With the points discussed in chapter 63, gradually your baby will love and anticipate sleep time and will settle independently to sleep. It just will not happen straightaway. Babies are born into a world that is completely new and foreign to them. They have come from a place where the temperature was consistent and where they had a continuous food source. Suddenly, when they are born, they enter an environment where they can see, smell, experience temperature changes, feel hunger or pain, etc. Work with your baby, and with what you feel your baby is telling you, so that all her needs are taken care of, and know that with time, patience and consistency everything will eventually work out. By 3 months, most babies 'chill-out'.

Grizzle

A grizzle is the cry of a baby who is winding down to sleep. A grizzle has gaps, and the tone and pitch vary. The gaps get longer as your baby starts to fall asleep. If you peek in on your baby who is winding down you will see a baby who shuts her eyes and nods off before grizzling again.

When a baby settles with little or no fuss, she may not grizzle at all or only briefly before going to sleep. When a baby settles to sleep with quite a bit of fuss, she may grizzle for longer.

When does my baby need help to go to sleep?

There will be times when your baby will need help to go to sleep, especially during the first few months. If her grizzling seems to be worsening rather than lessening, you may decide to help her get to sleep. There are no rights or wrongs here. Every parent/baby/situation is different. Different parents will choose different techniques, and at what point a parent chooses to implement a technique will also vary.

Emotional cry

If a baby cries emotionally, at any time, she needs to be attended to without delay. An emotional cry does not vary in pitch or tone (unlike a grizzle) and is continuous without gaps. In a young (and otherwise well) baby, an emotional cry is often attributed to lower wind pain, hunger or overtiredness. A baby crying emotionally should not be expected to settle to sleep on her own. If you feel that your baby is crying emotionally because of:

- Hunger, especially if her last feed was more than a couple of hours ago, or if you feel that her last feed was not as effective as usual, feed her. Remember that breastmilk is easily digested and it is normal for babies to have periods where they cluster feed (i.e. have shorter feeds more frequently). See chapter 1 for information on feeding cues
- Lower wind pain (see chapter 3 for cues on this), she is probably unsettled and will need a 'best-odds' method to be able to fall sleep (see chapter 72)
- Overtiredness (e.g. has been awake for much longer than the length of time a baby of similar age is generally capable of contentedly staying awake, see chapter 63 under 'Bedtime rituals'), she is probably unsettled and will require a 'best-odds' method to be able to fall sleep (see chapter 72).

Settling techniques

When your baby needs help to go off to sleep (there will be plenty of such times, especially in the early months), different techniques work best for different parents and different babies. And one technique which may work well on one occasion may not work the next.

Some parents may choose to implement a settling technique whereby a baby remains in her sleeping place. For example:

- Holding your baby's hands firmly into her chest
- Rhythmically patting your baby's nappy area
- Repetitively say 'Shhh'
- Any combination of the above

If one or more of the above techniques are going to work, they will probably begin to calm your baby within a few minutes. If they seem to be helping, continue them until her eyes start to become 'heavy'. If she begins to grizzle again soon after you stop, you may choose to start again immediately. If she stops grizzling for a little while, and then starts again, you may choose to listen to her grizzles for a while to see if she settles. If she does not, you may try the same technique again.

If the techniques listed above do not seem to be helping, put her over your shoulder. If she then burps and relaxes, the problem may have been upper wind pain (see chapter 3) and she may then settle to sleep.

If she still does not settle when over your shoulder, then repetitively pat her nappy area, or gently bob up and down (you can add 'Shhh' too). If this helps to relax and settle her, she may go to sleep.

For many babies, a calm 'top-up' breastfeed may be all that is needed. Sometimes a walk in the pram or a drive in the car can help.

If you find that things are dragging on and nothing seems to be helping settle your baby to sleep (or for only a short time), or you find that things are getting into an exhausting cycle of a short feed ⟷ short sleep, then she is probably unsettled (see chapter 72 below).

Sometimes babies go through stages (that last for days to weeks) of frequently fully waking around the 40-minute mark of their sleep and not resettling. This is not to be confused with a baby making sleeping sounds (see chapter 68 for clarification of sleeping sounds). Sometimes we just need to go with the flow here for a while and remain consistent (e.g. with bedtime rituals) because there may be nothing we can do to make her sleep longer, and eventually your baby will probably, all of a sudden, change back to her longer sleeps. These times may coincide with your baby having a 'growth spurt' or a 'wonder week' (see chapter 74) or when she is teething. Often during these times, your baby is grumpier than usual and her feeds become more frequent and sleeps become shorter.

PART 5

The Unsettled Baby

Unsettled Periods

What is an unsettled period?

During an unsettled period, your baby may cry frequently, be irritable, not settle well to sleep, cluster feed (see chapter 14 under 'Frequency of breastfeeds') and generally be 'out of sorts'. Around the time that her circadian rhythm begins to emerge (about 2 months) or a few weeks before, an unsettled period tends to begin in the late afternoon/early evening (known as the 'witching' or 'arsenic' hours). However, in the early weeks the unsettled periods tend to occur randomly.

How long do unsettled periods last?

Unsettled periods in a young baby are normal and transient. For the first couple of weeks, babies sleep a lot and crying periods are typically short and relatively easy to resolve. From 3 weeks, however, unsettled periods begin to emerge, just as babies are becoming more wakeful and active. From this time, one or two unsettled periods commonly occur every 24 hours in a young baby. Unsettled periods tend to peak at 6 weeks, before beginning to reduce from 2 months of age, and are usually resolved by around 3 months.[1]

Is there something 'wrong' with my baby?

Our society encourages the perception that babies who are loved, well cared for and well fed do not cry. It is no wonder that many parents are bewildered when, in spite of all their efforts, their baby continues to cry. This will often result in multiple visits to health professionals in search of a diagnosis and cure. Often, all that the health professional needs to do is actively listen and be supportive and encouraging, rather than provide a medical diagnosis or medication. This is especially important since unsettled behaviour in young babies is often mistakenly diagnosed, for example as gastro-oesophageal reflux disease (see chapter 38), lactose intolerance (see chapter 37) or a food sensitivity (see chapter 36). However, only 5% of unsettled babies actually have an organic disturbance.[2]

Why do unsettled periods occur?

No one knows for sure why young babies have these unsettled periods. However, many mothers will tell you that during these times their babies frequently display lower wind pain cues (see chapter 3). This would lend to the presumption that perhaps a young baby's immature digestive system may be associated with these unsettled periods.

Another theory is that, because after a month or so the unsettled periods have a tendency to begin in the late afternoon and/or early evening, they may be associated with the baby's central nervous system being overstimulated by this time, after having taken on a lot of stimuli during the day. At this time of the day a baby seeks comfort to help her regulate herself. So when she wants to cluster feed during this time, it is not just about the actual feeding; it is also about the close contact between a mother and her baby. This is how she processes what she has learnt during the day.

As a baby's circadian rhythm begins to emerge, she typically has her longest stretch of sleep during the first part of the night. For this reason, another theory is that unsettled periods tend to occur in the late afternoon/early evening as a way to obtain more feeds in a shorter time, as though she is 'tanking up' on higher fat/higher calorie-rich breastmilk (see chapter 10 under 'Are a breastfeeding mother's breasts ever completely empty?') to prepare for a longer sleep. (It is common for a baby to feed more frequently during an unsettled period.) This cluster feeding can form an important part of her overall nutritional needs for a 24-hour period.

What can I do to help my baby during unsettled periods?

To help settle your baby (and to help minimise the length of an unsettled period), it can help to implement a 'best-odds' method to get her off to sleep, a method that is safe and works for you.

Typically, a 'best-odds' method involves your baby being close to you. Human babies are born the most neurologically immature primate of all, with only 25% of their brain volume. Close human contact and proximity make it possible for a baby's brain to develop. And a mother's body is the only environment to which a baby is truly adapted.[3]

A baby has inherent responses to her mother's smell, movements and touch. When she is close to her mother, a baby's innate responses help her to:

- Reduce crying
- Regulate breathing
- Regulate body temperature
- Regulate metabolism
- Reduce stress levels
- Improve immune function
- Improve oxygen levels [4]

Methods which some parents find helpful to settle an unsettled baby include:

- Carrying her around in a sling or baby carrier
- Staying close (e.g. skin-to-skin) to her
- Taking her for a walk in the pram
- Moving the pram backwards and forwards over a small bump

Whatever technique you choose, it is important to give it a chance to work. It can take about 15 minutes to help get an unsettled baby to sleep. If you keep changing the strategy your baby will probably become more stimulated, and therefore increasingly unsettled.

Also, be prepared to stick with the 'best-odds' method for a while. If your baby is going to wake up refreshed, the sleep will need to be at least one complete cycle (i.e. at least one hour, see chapter 68). If you settle a baby to sleep during an unsettled period and then transfer her somewhere else, she probably will be awake crying again a short time later and the unsettled period will resume or persist.

So if your baby is under 3 months and has one or two unsettled periods every 24 hours (as described above), it is very likely that she is a normal healthy baby if she is:

- Growing normally (e.g. gaining weight well) and has a good output (see chapter 46)
- Otherwise her normal well self with no signs of illness (e.g. lethargy, vomiting, diarrhoea, cough, high temperature, poor feeding). See www.rch.org.au/kidsinfo/factsheets.cfm for more information on illness in children
- Meeting her developmental milestones (see www.raisingchildren. net.au for more information)

If you are concerned about your baby for any reason, seek medical advice.

As distressing as these unsettled periods can be, it is comforting to know that a longer stretch of sleep typically follows an unsettled period, and by about 3 months unsettled periods reduce and normally cease.

Co-Sleeping

Co-sleeping means that a mother and/or her partner sleeps on the same sleep surface (e.g. in the parents' bed) as the baby.

For the first 6 to 12 months, the safest place for your baby to sleep is in your room on a separate sleeping surface (e.g. a cot).[1]

However, if practised safely, some parents find co-sleeping can make breastfeeding easier during the night and can help everyone get more sleep. This is because when a baby is close to her mother, a mother can more quickly respond to her baby's cues. A baby is able to breastfeed whenever she needs to without the mother or the baby needing to wake fully. In this way, both mother and baby can settle back to sleep sooner.

Co-sleeping with a baby at least at some point overnight is common, even among parents who have no intention of co-sleeping with their baby before she is born.[2]

If you decide to share your bed with your baby, here are some points which will help ensure you do so safely:[3]

- Place your baby on her back to sleep
- Sleep facing your baby with your body curled around her to stop her from going under the covers or into a pillow
- Ensure the mattress is firm, flat and clean (waterbeds are not safe)
- Ensure that she cannot fall out of the bed, become trapped between the mattress and wall or be rolled on to
- Ensure that bedclothes (or anything else) cannot cover her face
- Do not wrap or swaddle your baby when co-sleeping because it can contribute to over-heating and it also restricts a baby's ability to move

Do not co-sleep with your baby: [4]

- If you or your partner smoke or if the mother smoked during pregnancy
- When either you or your partner is under the influence of alcohol or any drug (legal or illegal), or if either of you is extremely fatigued
- In the early months if your baby is born very small or premature
- On a sofa/couch/armchair/beanbag or similar (i.e. furniture not designed for sleeping on)
- If you are obese
- If persons other than the parents are present (e.g. a sibling or siblings)
- If a pet(s) is present
- If the baby is fed artificial milk

For more information on co-sleeping, consult a reputable source such as:

- SIDS and Kids information sheet *Sleeping with a baby*. Search for this at www.sidsandkids.org
- Australian Breastfeeding Association *Is your baby sleeping safely?* leaflet. Search for this at www.breastfeeding.asn.au
- UNICEF UK Baby Friendly Initiative leaflet *Caring for your baby at night*. This can be obtained from www.unicef.org.uk/ BabyFriendly/Resources/Resources-for-parents/Caring-for-your-baby-at-night/.

Is it a Growth Spurt or a Wonder Week?

At times you will find that your baby will not be her usual self. She will generally be more irritable, want to feed more frequently and have shorter sleeps, especially during the day (e.g. she will have many 40-minute sleeps). These fussy times often occur every few weeks for the first 6 months or so, and then every few months thereafter into toddlerhood. They typically last from a few days to a few weeks.

Some classify these fussy times as growth spurts, when it is believed that a baby is hungrier because of sudden, rapid growth. Be assured that if this is the case, by feeding your baby more frequently over a few days your milk supply will increase and will match the growth spurt.[1]

Other times when a baby may feed more frequently include:
- During warm weather
- If she has been exposed to a virus, as a way to boost her immune defences by receiving more antibodies from her mother's milk

Others classify these fussy times as a 'wonder week', a time when major changes occur in babies' brains. Each major change represents a leap forward in your baby's mental development when more synaptic connections are being made in her brain.[2]

Those with older babies or toddlers will often classify these fussy times as a time when she is teething.

Whatever they are caused by, all mothers will tell you that they exist. It can at least be comforting to know that they are usually normal and just a brief phase, as long as your baby is developing and growing normally and showing no signs of illness (as described in chapter 72 above). Try as much as you can to remain calm and consistent during these times, and know that things will eventually get back on track.

Once again, if you are concerned for any reason, seek medical advice.

PART 6

Useful Resources

Useful Resources

Helpful breastfeeding websites:
- www.breastfeeding.asn.au
- www.kellymom.com
- www.nbci.ca
- www.breastfeedingonline.com

International Board Certified Lactation Consultant (IBCLC) websites:
- www.lcanz.org (lactation consultants in Australia/New Zealand)
- www.ilca.org (lactation consultants around the world)
- www.lactation.org.au (lactation consultants in Victoria)
- www.lactationwest.org.au (lactation consultants in Western Australia)

Other useful websites:
- PANDA (post- (and ante-) natal depression support/advice) www.panda.org.au
- Dietitians Association of Australia www.daa.asn.au
- National Health and Medical Research Council www.nhmrc.gov.au
- Eat For Health www.eatforhealth.gov.au
- World Health Organization www.who.int
- Raising Children Network www.raisingchildren.net.au
- Royal Children's Hospital Melbourne Kids Health Information for Parents www.rch.org.au/kidsinfo/factsheets.cfm
- SIDS and Kids www.sidsandkids.org

Useful telephone contacts:

- PANDA (post- (and ante-) natal depression support/advice) 1300 726 306
- Australian Breastfeeding Association's National Breastfeeding Helpline 1800 686 268 (1800 mum 2 mum) (24-hour breastfeeding information line)
- Monash Medical Centre Pregnancy and Breastfeeding Drug Information line (Victoria), 03 9594 2361
- Mothersafe, Royal Hospital for Women Pregnancy and Breastfeeding Drug Information line (NSW), 02 9382 6539
- Medicines Information Centre, Canberra Hospital, Pregnancy and Breastfeeding Drug Information line (ACT), 02 6244 3333
- Women and Newborn Health Services (KEMH), Pregnancy and Breastfeeding Drug Information line (WA), 08 9340 2723
- Health Direct (24-hour health advice line) 1800 022 222 (most states in Australia)
- 24-hour maternal health line 132 229 (Victoria only)
- 13Health Health services advice line 13 432584 (Queensland only)

Useful books

- *The Breastfeeding Mothers Guide to Making More Milk* (2009) by Diana West (International Board Certified Lactation Consultant) and Lisa Marasco (International Board Certified Lactation Consultant) – a valuable book about milk-supply concerns
- *Baby-led Weaning* (2008) by Gill Rapley and Tracey Murkett – a valuable book about introducing family foods (complementary/ solid foods)

Note for New Zealand readers

New Zealand readers are also directed to the:

- La Leche League website for breastfeeding information and support www.lalecheleague.org.nz/
- SIDS New Zealand website for information about safe sleeping sids.org.nz/
- Ministry of Health website for information on many areas of health www.health.govt.nz/
- Baby Friendly Initiative for Aotearoa New Zealand www.babyfriendly.org.nz/
- Women's Health Action Trust New Zealand www.womens-health.org.nz/

Epilogue ... from a Baby's Perspective

Dear Mummy,

I cannot tell you, Mummy, how excited I was to finally meet you. From the first time I laid my eyes on you, I knew that I was in love. That skin-to-skin time with you after I was born, and in the early weeks, was magical. It really helped to lead me where I needed to go. Thank you so much for breastfeeding me! I'm sure you know that your milk is made just for me.

Mummy, I know that you are really tired and that sometimes you get upset because taking care of me seems so hard, but before you give up on feeding me this yummy milk, let me tell you all about me. Hopefully it will make you feel better.

I'm really good at letting you know when I need some more breastmilk. I turn my head from side to side with my mouth open, stick my tongue out, become a bit restless, make some squeaky noises and bring my hands to my mouth. I know that Grandma sometimes says "How can she be hungry again? She just fed", but your milk is awesome stuff, Mummy. I can digest it so well that it makes me poo a lot (sorry about that), and my tummy is really small so it doesn't stay full for very long, so I feel like I need to feed again – sometimes even an hour after I last fed!

I know it seems really confusing that sometimes I want to suck all the time and sometimes you think "How can there be anything left?" and "Surely you are not drinking any more!" But please know that if I ever feel like I need more milk, I can always get it from you – I'm really good at that. In fact, nothing, not even the best breast pump, can get milk from your breasts in the way that I can.

I am also very good at regulating what I need, so please don't worry about overfeeding me. Sometimes I will suck and swallow to get your milk. Other times I will just suck – like I'm savouring a bowl of ice cream ... You know how sometimes you scrape just a tiny bit on to your spoon because you want it to last a long time? You are better than ice cream though!

The good news is that because I suckled so often in the early weeks, it made your body do all these clever things so you keep making exactly the right amount of milk for as long as you breastfeed me. That's so cool.

Mummy, I know that I can make you really frustrated when I go through one of my unsettled periods. I'm really sorry about this. It's just that my tummy feels sore and my head feels like it has too much going on inside it. I can't see much, and everything that I hear and feel is so different from how I remember when I was inside you.

I'm sorry that I cry so much during my unsettled periods. I know that you are doing everything you can to try to help me, and please know that you are helping me. I won't always be like this, Mummy. My tummy and brain just need time to mature. Sometimes crying and sucking are just how I make sense of everything. It's difficult to describe. During these times, there is nowhere I'd rather be than in yours or Daddy's arms. Hearing yours or Daddy's voice and smelling your smell makes me feel so much better.

Mummy, at the moment I'm sorry that I wake you up lots throughout the night. I have no idea when it is daytime or night-time. My body doesn't let me sleep for very long – I keep waking up a lot and I feel like I want to do more sucking at your breast. When I was inside you, I never had these feelings. I had food all the time, but now I get these strange sensations in my tummy telling me that I need to suckle more. And once I do I feel so much better.

The good news is that with time I will gradually sleep for longer at night and probably even settle really well at night. You are doing a great job at teaching me the difference between day and night, Mummy, by keeping things quiet and dark at night, and bright for my awake times during the day.

I also like it how you are trying to get me used to spending some time on my tummy during my awake times, and how you let my bottom get some air. Thanks, Mummy. You are the best.

That bedtime ritual that you have started really helps, and the massage you give me after my bath feels so lovely. I am learning to look forward to sleep time. And I love it when you hold me close and sing to me. Everyone else says your singing is lousy, but to me, you and your voice are perfect.

Mummy, it really helps too when you pick me up when I'm telling you that I'm tired and you let me have a sleep. When my body is starting to get tense and my movements are becoming jerky and I start to become uninterested in what's going on and I start to frown or stare, and yawn, I really need a sleep. If I stay awake too long after this my head feels all fuzzy and I find that I need to cry a lot to get my emotions out, and although I'm really tired I cannot seem to go to sleep easily. This is when I really like to stay close to you.

I know that it is frustrating and confusing, and it even can make you doubt yourself, when people ask you "Is she sleeping through yet?" And I know that it is really tiring for you to feed me during the night, but I promise I won't always wake you up. For now though, my body is just not ready to sleep through. Sometimes I wake because I'm hungry and other times I feel like I just need some time to be close to you and suckle. And at night there are no distractions like there are during the day. It's like I have you all to myself and can gaze into your beautiful eyes, smell your beautiful smell, feel your beautiful warmth and skin, listen to your breath and heartbeat and, of course, drink some of your awesome milk.

Mummy, you know how Daddy and you were sick last week? Well, your breastmilk made it so that I didn't get sick. My body told me that I needed to feed more so that I could get more of those precious antibodies from your milk, and so I didn't get sick! Thank you. Your breastmilk is helping me grow and develop in the most perfect way. There is absolutely nothing that comes close to it.

Mummy, I know you are trying your very best for me and you have been worried about whether you are making enough milk for me. I know that it is hard because you cannot measure how much milk I get at each feed. Even a breast pump cannot tell you, because not even the best pump in the world can mimic how I get your milk.

I know you're very busy, and important, and there's so much you used to do before I was born. I know that right now it feels like you'll never do those things again, and our house is getting messy and this makes you anxious. But please know, every moment you spend holding me, every time you gaze into my eyes, and every hour you spend breastfeeding, is so important to me, because you are all that I know. I love Daddy and Grandma and all of our other family and friends, but I'm happiest and least stressed when I'm with you.

Mummy, I will make you a promise. I can't say exactly when, but the time will come when I will need you a little less intensely, and when I will sleep more at night and settle to sleep really well. But for now, I need you. Thank you for everything. I hope that my cuddles, cheeky smiles and giggles will keep you going!

I love you, Mummy.

Baby

References

INTRODUCTION

1. World Health Organization 2011, *Exclusive breastfeeding for six months best for babies everywhere*, Geneva: World Health Organization. Accessed 19/2/12 from www.who.int/mediacentre/news/statements/2011/breastfeeding_20110115/en/index.html

2. Australian Institute of Health and Welfare 2011, *2010 Australian National Infant Feeding Survey: indicator results*, Canberra: AIHW. Accessed 19/2/12 from www.aihw.gov.au/publication-detail/?id=10737420927

3. Perrine CG, Scanlon KS, Odom E, Grummer-Strawn LM 2012, *Baby-friendly hospital practices and meeting exclusive breastfeeding intention*, Pediatrics, 130(1):54-60.

4. Australian Health Ministers' Conference 2009, *The Australian National Breastfeeding Strategy 2010-2015*. Australian Government Department of Health and Ageing, Canberra. Accessed 8/12/12 from www.health.gov.au/internet/main/publishing.nsf/Content/aust-breastfeeding-strategy-2010-2015.

CHAPTER 1

1. Dunstan P 2006-2010, *Understanding the meaning of your baby's cries*. Accessed 15/2/12 from www.dunstanbaby.com/cms/index.php?page=au-home

CHAPTER 2

1. Dunstan P 2006-2010, *Understanding the meaning of your baby's cries*. Accessed 15/2/12 from www.dunstanbaby.com/cms/index.php?page=au-home

CHAPTER 3

1. Dunstan P 2006-2010, *Understanding the meaning of your baby's cries*. Accessed 15/2/12 from www.dunstanbaby.com/cms/index.php?page=au-home

2. Ibid.

CHAPTER 4

1. Blair PS, Mitchell EA, Heckstall-Smith EM, Fleming PJ 2008, *Head covering - a major modifiable risk factor for sudden infant death syndrome: a systematic review*, Archives of Disease in Childhood, 93(9):778-783.

2. Dunstan P 2006-2010, *Understanding the meaning of your baby's cries*. Accessed 15/2/12 from www.dunstanbaby.com/cms/index.php?page=au-home

CHAPTER 5

1. World Health Organization 2011, *Exclusive breastfeeding for six months best for babies everywhere*, Geneva: World Health Organization. Accessed 19/2/12 from www.who.int/mediacentre/news/statements/2011/breastfeeding_20110115/en/index.html

2. National Health and Medical Research Council 2012, *Infant Feeding Guidelines*, Canberra: National Health and Medical Research Council. Accessed 18/2/13 www.eatforhealth.gov.au

3. World Health Organization 2012, *Breastfeeding – exclusive breastfeeding*, Geneva: World Health Organization. Accessed 12/12/12 from www.who.int/elena/titles/exclusive_breastfeeding/en/

4. Cattaneo A, Ronfani L, Burmaz T, Quintero-Romero S, Macaluso A, Di Mario S 2006, *Infant feeding and cost of health care: a cohort study*, Acta Paediatr 95(5):540-546.

   Smith JP, Thompson JF, Ellwood DA 2002, *Hospital system costs of artificial infant feeding: estimates for the Australian Capital Territory*, The Australian and New Zealand Journal of Public Health 26(6):543-551.

5. Van der Wijden C, Brown J, Kleijen J 2003, *Lactational amenorrhea for family planning*, Cochrane Database of Systematic Reviews 4:CD001329.

6. World Health Organization publication, *Lactational amenorrhea method (LAM)*. Accessed 11/12/12 from www.who.int/reproductivehealth/publications/family_planning/9241593229/en/

CHAPTER 6

1. Ip S, Chung M, Raman G, Chew P, Magula N, DeVine D, et al 2007, *Breastfeeding and Maternal and Infant Health Outcomes in Developed Countries*, Rockville, MD: Agency for Healthcare Research and Quality.

2. Ibid.

3. Hauck FR, Thompson JM, Tanabe KO, Moon RY, Vennemann MM 2011, *Breastfeeding and reduced risk of sudden infant death syndrome: a meta-analysis*, Pediatrics 128(1):103-110.

4. Ip S, Chung M, Raman G, Chew P, Magula N, DeVine D, et al 2007, *Breastfeeding and Maternal and Infant Health Outcomes in Developed Countries*, Rockville, MD: Agency for Healthcare Research and Quality.

5. Ibid.

6. Ibid.

7. Akobeng AK, Ramanan AV, Buchan I, Heller RF 2010, *Effect of breast-feeding on risk of coeliac disease: a systematic review and meta-analysis of observational studies*, Archives of Disease in Childhood 91(1):39-43.

8. Julvez J, Ribas-Fito N, Forns M, Garcia-Esteban R, Torrent M, Sunyer J 2007, *Attention behaviour and hyperactivity at age 4 and duration of breast-feeding*, Acta Paediatrica 96(6):842-847.

9. Sorensen HJ, Mortensen EL, Reinisch JM, Mednick SA 2005, *Breastfeeding and risk of schizophrenia in the Copenhagen Perinatal Cohort*, Acta Psychiatric Scandinavia 112(1):26-29.

10. Horta BL, Bahl R, Martines JC, Victora CG 2007, *Evidence on the long term effects of breastfeeding: systematic reviews and meta-analyses*, Geneva: World Health Organization.

11. Ibid.

12. Ibid.

13. Ibid.

14. Mimouni Bloch A, Mimouni D, Mimouni M, Gdalevich M 2002, *Does breastfeeding protect against allergic rhinitis during childhood?* A meta-analysis of prospective studies, Acta Paediatra 91(3):275-279.

15. Gdalevich M, Mimouni D, David M, Mimouni M 2001, *Breast-feeding and the onset of atopic dermatitis in childhood: a systematic review and meta-analysis of prospective studies,* Journal American Academy Dermatology 45(4):520-527.

16. Jedrychowski W, Perera F, Jankowski J, Butscher M, Mroz E, Flak E, et al 2011, *Effect of exclusive breastfeeding on the development of children's cognitive function in the Krakow prospective birth cohort study,* European Journal of Pediatrics, Electronic Publication June 10, 2011.

    Kramer MS, Matush L, Vanilovich I, Platt RW, Bogdanovich N, Sevkovskaya Z, et al 2008, *Breastfeeding and child cognitive development. New evidence from a large randomised trial,* Archives General Psychiatry 65(5):578-584.

    Quigley MA, Hockley C, Carson C, Kelly Y, Renfrew MJ, Sacker A 2011, *Breastfeeding is Associated with Improved Child Cognitive Development: A Population-Based Cohort Study,* Journal of Pediatrics, Electronic Publication August 10, 2011.

17. Horta, BL, Bahl, R, Martines, JC, & Victora, CG 2007, *Evidence on the long term effects of breastfeeding: systematic reviews and meta-analyses,* Geneva: World Health Organization.

18. Arnold R, Cole M, McGhee J 1997, *A bactericidal effect for human lactoferrin,* Science 197:263-265.

    Erickson PR, McClintock KL, Green N, et al 1998, *Estimation of the caries-related risk associated with infant formulas,* Pediatric Dentistry 20:395-403.

    Mandel ID 1996, *Caries prevention: current strategies, new directions,* JADA 127:1477-1488.

    Ribeiro NM, Ribeiro MA 2004, *Breastfeeding and early childhood caries:* a critical review, Jornal de Pediatria 80(5 Suppl):S199-S210.

    Rugg-Gunn A, Roberts GJ, Wright WG 1985, *Effect of human milk on plaque pH in situ and enamel dissolution in vitro compared with bovine milk, lactose, and sucrose,* Caries Research 19:327-334.

19. Ip S, Chung M, Raman G, Chew P, Magula N, DeVine D, et al 2007, Breastfeeding and Maternal and Infant Health Outcomes in Developed Countries, Rockville, MD: Agency for Healthcare Research and Quality.

    Zheng T, Duan L, Liu Y, Zhang B, Wang Y, Chen T, Zhang Y, Owens PH 2000, *Lactation reduces breast cancer risk in Shandong Province, China,* American Journal of Epidemiology 152(12):1129-1135.

20. Ip S, Chung M, Raman G, Chew P, Magula N, DeVine D, et al 2007, *Breastfeeding and Maternal and Infant Health Outcomes in Developed Countries,* Rockville, MD: Agency for Healthcare Research and Quality.

21. Ibid.

22. Karlson EW, Mandl LA, Hankinson SE, Grodstein F 2004, *Breastfeeding reduces the risk of rheumatoid arthritis,* Arthritis and rheumatism 50(11):3458-3467.

23. Schnatz PF, Barker KG, Marakovits KA, O'Sullivan DM 2010, *Effects of age at first pregnancy and breast-feeding on the development of postmenopausal osteoporosis*, Menopause 17(6):1161-1166.

24. Krause KM, Lovelady CA, Peterson BL, Chowdhury N, Østbye T 2010, *Effect of breast-feeding on weight retention at 3 and 6 months postpartum: data from the North Carolina WIC Programme*, Public Health Nutrition 13(12):2019-2026.

CHAPTER 7

1. Araújo ED, Gonçalves AK, Cornetta MC, Cunha H, Cardoso ML, Morais SS, et al 2005, *Evaluation of the secretory immunoglobulin A levels in the colostrum and milk of mothers of term and pre-term newborns*, The Brazilian Journal of Infectious Diseases 9(5):357-362.

   Bokor S, Koletzko B, Decsi T 2007, *Systematic review of fatty acid composition of human milk from mothers of preterm compared to full-term infants*, Annals of Nutrition & Metabolism 51(6):550-556.

   Ronayne de Ferrer PA, Baroni A, Sambucetti ME, López NE, Ceriani Cernadas JM 2000, *Lactoferrin levels in term and preterm milk*, Journal of the American College of Nutrition 19(3):370-373.

2. Rechtman DJ, Lee ML, Berg H 2006, *Effect of Environmental Conditions on Unpasteurized Donor Human Milk*, Breastfeeding Medicine 1(1):24-26.

3. Riordan J 2010, *The Biological Specificity of Breastmilk* (Chapter 4). In Riordan J, & Wambach K (Eds), *Breastfeeding and human lactation* (4th ed), Sudbury: Jones and Bartlett Publishers.

4. Jensen RG 1999, *Lipids in human milk*, Lipids 34(12):1243.

   Sala-Vila A, Castellote AI, Rodriguez-Palmero M, Campoy C, López-Sabater MC 2005, *Lipid composition in human breastmilk from Granada (Spain): Changes during lactation*, Nutrition 21(4):467–473.

5. Owen CD, Whincup PH, Odoki K, Gilg JA, Cook DG 2002, *Infant feeding and blood cholesterol: a study in adolescents and a systematic review*, Pediatrics 110(3):597-608.

6. Wagner V, Stockhausen JG 1988, *The effect of feeding human milk and adapted milk formulae on serum lipid and lipoprotein levels in young infants*, European Journal of Pediatrics 147(3):292-295.

7. Riordan J 2010, *The Biological Specificity of Breastmilk* (Chapter 4). In Riordan J & Wambach K (Eds), *Breastfeeding and human lactation* (4th ed), Sudbury: Jones and Bartlett Publishers.

8. Ibid.

9. Woodford K 2010, *Devil in the milk. Illness, health and politics. A1 and A2 milk*, New Zealand: Craig Potton Publishing.

10. Kaminski S, Cieslinska A, Kostyra E 2007, *Polymorphism of bovine beta-casein and its potential effect on human health*, Journal of Applied Genetics 48(3):189-198.

11. Brantl V 1984, *Novel opioid peptides derived from human beta-casein: human beta-casomorphins*, European Journal of Pharmacology 106(1):213-214.

12. Wasilewska J, Sienkiewicz-Szlapka E, Kuzbida E, Jarmolowska B, Kaczmarski M, Kostyra E 2011, *The exogenous opioid peptides and DPPIV serum activity in infants with apnoea*

expressed as apparent life threatening events (ALTE), Neuropeptides 45(3):189-195.

13. Riordan J 2010, *The Biological Specificity of Breastmilk* (Chapter 4). In Riordan J & Wambach K (Eds), *Breastfeeding and human lactation* (4th ed), Sudbury: Jones and Bartlett Publishers.

CHAPTER 10

1. Neville MC, McFadden TB, Forsyth I 2002, *Hormonal Regulation of Mammary Differentiation and Milk Secretion*, Journal of Mammary Gland Biology and Neoplasia 7(1):49-66.

2. Kim JY, Mizoguchi Y, Yamaguchi H, Enami J, Sakai S 1997, *Removal of milk by suckling acutely increases the prolactin receptor gene expression in the lactating mouse mammary gland*, Molecular and Cellular Endocrinology 131(1):31-38.

    Theil P, Seirsen K, Hurley WL, Labouriau R, Thomsen B, Sorensen MT 2006, *Role of suckling in regulating cell turnover and onset and maintenance of lactation in individual mammary glands of sows*, Journal of Animal Science 84(7):1691-1698.

3. Kent JC, Leon MR, Cregan MD, Ramsay DT, Doherty DA, Hartmann PE 2006, *Volume and Frequency of Breastfeedings and Fat Content of Breastmilk Throughout the Day*, Pediatrics 117(3):e387-e395.

4. Kent JC 2007, *How Breastfeeding Works*, Journal of Midwifery & Women's Health 52(6):564-570.

5. Kent JC, Leon MR, Cregan MD, Ramsay DT, Doherty DA, Hartmann PE 2006, *Volume and Frequency of Breastfeedings and Fat Content of Breastmilk Throughout the Day*, Pediatrics 117(3):e387-e395.

6. Ibid.

7. Kent JC 2007, *How Breastfeeding Works*, Journal of Midwifery & Women's Health 52(6):564-570.

8. Sachdev HP, Krishna J, Puri RK 1992, *Do exclusively breast fed infants need fluid supplementation?* Indian Pediatrics 29(4):535-540.

    National Health and Medical Research Council 2012, *Infant Feeding Guidelines*, Canberra: National Health and Medical Research Council. Accessed 18/2/13 www.eatforhealth.gov.au

9. Szajewska H, Horvath A, Koletzko B, Kalisz M 2006, *Effects of brief exposure to water, breast-milk substitutes, or other liquids on the success and duration of breastfeeding: a systematic review*, Acta Paediatrica 95(2):145-152.

CHAPTER 11

1. Ramsay DT, Kent JC, Owens RA, Hartmann PE 2004, *Ultrasound imaging of milk ejection in the breast of lactating women*, Pediatrics 113(2):361-367.

2. Ibid.

3. Kent JC, Geddes DT, Hepworth AR, Hartmann PE 2011, *Effect of Warm Breastshields on Breast Milk Pumping*, Journal of Human Lactation 27(4):331-338.

CHAPTER 14

1. Kent JC, Leon MR, Cregan MD, Ramsay DT, Doherty DA, Hartmann PE 2006, *Volume and Frequency of Breastfeedings and Fat Content of Breastmilk Throughout the Day*, Pediatrics 117(3):e387-e395.

CHAPTER 16

1. Coates MM 2010, *Tides in breastfeeding practice* (Chapter 2). In Riordan J & Wambach K (Eds), *Breastfeeding and human lactation* (4th ed), Sudbury: Jones and Bartlett Publishers.

2. Smillie CM 2008, *How infants learn to feed: A neurobehavioural model*, In Watson Genna C, *Supporting suckling skills in breastfeeding infants*, Sudbury: Jones and Bartlett Publishers.

3. Newman J, Pitman T 2006, *The latch and other keys to breastfeeding success*, Texas: Hale Publishing.

4. Sinusas K, Gagliardi A 2001, *Initial management of breastfeeding*, American Family Physician 64:981-988.

5. Colson S 2010, *An Introduction to Biological Nurturing*, Texas: Hale Publishing

6. Walker M 2006, *Breastfeeding management for the clinician: using the evidence*, Sudbury: Jones and Bartlett Publishers.

7. Smillie CM 2008, *How infants learn to feed: A neurobehavioural model*, In Watson Genna C, Supporting suckling skills in breastfeeding infants, Sudbury: Jones and Bartlett Publishers.

8. Moore ER, Anderson GC, Bergman N 2009, *Early skin-to-skin contact for mothers and their healthy newborn infants*, The Cochrane Library 1:1-41.

   Rashad WA, Mahmoud NS 2009, *Effect of maternal-neonate skin to skin contact on the neonates thermoregulation*, Alexandria Bulletin 45:311-314.

CHAPTER 17

1. Dewey KG, Nommsen-Rivers LA, Heinig JM, Cohen RJ 2003, *Risk Factors for Suboptimal Infant Breastfeeding Behavior, Delayed Onset of Lactation, and Excess Neonatal Weight Loss*, Pediatrics 112:607.

   Sinusas K, Gagliardi A 2001, *Initial management of breastfeeding*, American Family Physician 64:981-988.

2. Newman J, Pitman T 2006, *The latch and other keys to breastfeeding success*, Texas: Hale Publishing.

3. Colson SD, Meek JH, Hawdon JM 2008, *Optimal positions for the release of primitive neonatal reflexes stimulating breastfeeding*, Early Human Development 84:441-449.

4. Smillie CM 2008, *How infants learn to feed: A neurobehavioural model*, In Watson Genna C, *Supporting suckling skills in breastfeeding infants*, Sudbury: Jones and Bartlett Publishers.

5. Pitman T 2011, 0-1 year: *Breastfeeding positions*, Today's Parent 28:107-108.

   Colson, S., (2010), *An Introduction to Biological Nurturing*, Texas: Hale Publishing.

CHAPTER 18

1. Chirico G, Marzollo R, Cortinovis S, Fonte C, Gasparoni A 2008, *Antiinfective Properties of Human Milk*, The Journal of Nutrition 138(9):1801S-1806S.

CHAPTER 20

1. National Health and Medical Research Council 2012, *Infant Feeding Guidelines*, Canberra: National Health and Medical Research Council. Accessed 18/2/13 www.eatforhealth.gov.au

CHAPTER 22

1. National Health and Medical Research Council 2012, *Infant Feeding Guidelines*, Canberra: National Health and Medical Research Council. Accessed 18/2/13 www.eatforhealth.gov.au

CHAPTER 23

1. Abou-Dakn M, Fluhr JW, Gensch M, Wöckel A 2011, *Positive Effect of HPA Lanolin versus Expressed Breastmilk on Painful and Damaged Nipples during Lactation*, Skin Pharmacology and Physiology 24:27–35.

CHAPTER 26

1. Joanna Briggs Institute 2009, *The management of nipple pain and/or trauma associated with breastfeeding*, Australian Nursing Journal 17(2):32–35.

2. Ibid.

CHAPTER 27

1. World Health Organization publication 2000, *Mastitis Causes and Management*, Geneva: World Health Organization. Accessed 23/3/12 from whqlibdoc.who.int/hq/2000/WHO_FCH_CAH_00.13.pdf

2. Ibid.

3. The Academy of Breastfeeding Medicine Protocol Committee 2008, *ABM Clinical Protocol #4: Mastitis Revision*, Breastfeeding Medicine 3(3):177-180.

4. The Academy of Breastfeeding Medicine Protocol Committee 2008, *ABM Clinical Protocol #4: Mastitis Revision*, Breastfeeding Medicine 3(3):177-180.

   Texas Department of Health/Bureau of Nutrition Services 2001, *Normal Breast Fullness, Engorgement, Plugged Ducts and Breast Infections*, Fact sheet number 22.

   World Health Organization publication 2000, *Mastitis Causes and Management*, Geneva: World Health Organization. Accessed 23/3/12 from whqlibdoc.who.int/hq/2000/WHO_FCH_CAH_00.13.pdf

5. World Health Organization publication 2000, *Mastitis Causes and Management*, Geneva: World Health Organization. Accessed 23/3/12 from whqlibdoc.who.int/hq/2000/WHO_FCH_CAH_00.13.pdf

6. Ibid.

   Texas Department of Health/Bureau of Nutrition Services 2001, *Normal Breast Fullness, Engorgement, Plugged Ducts and Breast Infections*, Fact sheet number 22.

   World Health Organization publication 2000, *Mastitis Causes and Management*, Geneva: World Health Organization. Accessed 23/3/12 from whqlibdoc.who.int/hq/2000/

WHO_FCH_CAH_00.13.pdf

7. Brodribb W, Fallon AB, Jackson C, Hegney D 2009, *Breastfeeding knowledge - the experiences of Australian general practice registrars*, Australian Family Physician 38(1-2):26-29.

CHAPTER 28

1. Lawlor-Smith L, Lawlor-Smith C 1997, Vasospasm of the nipple–a manifestation of Raynaud's phenomenon: case reports, British Medical Journal 314(7081):644–645.

2. Kernerman E, Newman J 2009, *Vasospasm and Raynaud's Phenomenon*. Accessed 12/12/12 from www.nbci.ca/index.php?option=com_content&view=article&id=52:vasospasm-and-raynauds-phenomenon&catid=5:information&Itemid=17

3. Anderson JE, Held N, Wright K 2004, *Raynaud's Phenomenon of the Nipple: A Treatable Cause of Painful Breastfeeding*, Pediatrics 113(4):e360-e364.

4. Anderson JE, Held N, Wright K 2004, *Raynaud's Phenomenon of the Nipple: A Treatable Cause of Painful Breastfeeding*, Pediatrics 113(4):e360-e364.

    Lawlor-Smith L, Lawlor-Smith C 1997, Vasospasm of the nipple–a manifestation of Raynaud's phenomenon: case reports, British Medical Journal 314(7081):644–645.

CHAPTER 29

1. National Health and Medical Research Council 2012, *Infant Feeding Guidelines*, Canberra: National Health and Medical Research Council. Accessed 18/2/13 www.eatforhealth.gov.au

    World Health Organization publication 2009, *Infant and young child feeding: model chapter for textbooks for medical students and allied health professionals*, Geneva: World Health Organization. Accessed 19/2/12 from whqlibdoc.who.int/publications/2009/9789241597494_eng.pdf

    Amir LH, Cullinane M, Garland SM, Tabrizi SN, Donat SM, Bennett CM, et al 2011, *The role of micro-organisms (Staphylococcus aureus and Candida albicans) in the pathogenesis of breast pain and infection in lactating women: study protocol*, Biomedical Central Pregnancy and Childbirth 11(54):1-10.

2. World Health Organization publication 2009, *Infant and young child feeding: model chapter for textbooks for medical students and allied health professionals*, Geneva: World Health Organization. Accessed 19/2/12 from whqlibdoc.who.int/publications/2009/9789241597494_eng.pdf

3. Amir LH 2003, *Breast pain in lactating women – mastitis or something else?* Australian Family Physician 32(3):1-5.

    The Royal Women's Hospital 2004, *Breastfeeding: Thrush in Lactation* clinical practice guideline. Accessed 2/1/13 from www.thewomens.org.au/BreastfeedingClinicalPracticeGuidelines

    Wiener S 2006, *Diagnosis and Management of Candida of the Nipple and Breast*, Journal of Midwifery & Women's Health 51(2):125–128.

4. National Health and Medical Research Council 2012, *Infant Feeding Guidelines*, Canberra: National Health and Medical Research Council. Accessed 18/2/13 www.eatforhealth.gov.au

5. Amir LH 2003, *Breast pain in lactating women – mastitis or something else?* Australian Family Physician 32(3):1-5.

6. Amir LH, Cullinane M, Garland SM, Tabrizi SN, Donat SM, Bennett CM, et al 2011, *The role of micro-organisms (Staphylococcus aureus and Candida albicans) in the pathogenesis of breast pain and infection in lactating women: study protocol*, Biomedical Central Pregnancy and Childbirth 11(54):1-10.

The Academy of Breastfeeding Medicine Protocol Committee 2008, *ABM Clinical Protocol #4: Mastitis Revision*, Breastfeeding Medicine 3(3):177-180.

7. Hafner-Eaton C 1997, *Breast yeast*, Midwifery Today 42:37-39, 68-69, 71.

8. Betzold CM 2007, *Update on the Recognition and Management of Lactational Breast Inflammation: Infections of the Nipple*, Journal of Midwifery & Women's Health 52(6):595-605.

9. Heritage J, Evans EGV, Killington RA 1999, *Microbiology in Action*, Cambridge, UK: Cambridge University Press.

10. Newman J 2011, *Candida protocol*. Accessed 9/2/12 from www.breastfeedinginc.ca/content.php?pagename=doc-CP

Wiener S 2006, *Diagnosis and Management of Candida of the Nipple and Breast*, Journal of Midwifery & Women's Health 51(2):125-128.

11. The Academy of Breastfeeding Medicine Protocol Committee 2010, *ABM Clinical Protocol #8: Human Milk Storage Information for Home Use for Full-Term Infants*, Breastfeeding Medicine 5(3):127-130.

CHAPTER 30

1. World Health Organization publication 2000, *Mastitis Causes and Management*, Geneva: World Health Organization. Accessed 23/3/12 from whqlibdoc.who.int/hq/2000/WHO_FCH_CAH_00.13.pdf

CHAPTER 31

1. National Health and Medical Research Council 2012, *Infant Feeding Guidelines*, Canberra: National Health and Medical Research Council. Accessed 18/2/13 www.eatforhealth.gov.au

CHAPTER 32

1. Cohen SM 2006, *Jaundice in the Full-Term Newborn*, Pediatric Nursing 32(3):202-208.

World Health Organization publication 2009, *Infant and young child feeding: model chapter for textbooks for medical students and allied health professionals*, Geneva: World Health Organization. Accessed 24/3/12 from whqlibdoc.who.int/publications/2009/9789241597494_eng.pdf

2. World Health Organization publication 2009, *Infant and young child feeding: model chapter for textbooks for medical students and allied health professionals*, Geneva: World Health Organization. Accessed 24/3/12 from http://whqlibdoc.who.int/publications/2009/9789241597494_eng.pdf

3. Newman J, Pitman T 2009, *Dr Jack Newman's Guide to Breastfeeding*, New York: HarperCollins Publishers Ltd.

American Academy of Pediatics (subcommittee on hyperbilirubinemia) 2004, *Management of Hyperbilirubinemia in the Newborn Infant 35 or More Weeks of Gestation*, Pediatrics 114(1):297-316.

4. Newman J, Pitman T 2009, *Dr Jack Newman's Guide to Breastfeeding*, New York: HarperCollins Publishers Ltd.

CHAPTER 33

1. Hamosh M, et al 1991, *Nutrition During Lactation*, Institute of Medicine, Washington DC: National Academy Press.

   Parpia Khan SL 2004, *Maternal Nutrition during Breastfeeding*, New Beginnings 21(2):44.

2. Ibid.

3. Ibid.

4. Kent JC 2007, *How Breastfeeding Works*, Journal of Midwifery & Women's Health 52(6):564-570.

5. Hausner H, Bredie WL, Mølgaard C, Petersen MA, Møller P 2008, *Differential transfer of dietary flavour compounds into human breastmilk*, Physiology and Behaviour 95(1-2):118-124.

6. Shim JE, Kim J, Mathai RA 2011, *Associations of Infant Feeding Practices and Picky Eating Behaviors of Preschool Children*, Journal of the American Dietetic Association 111(9):1363-1368.

CHAPTER 34

1. Kent JC 2007, *How Breastfeeding Works*, Journal of Midwifery & Women's Health 52(6):564-570.

2. Ibid.

3. Ibid.

4. Mann J, Truswell S (Eds) 2002, *Essentials of Human Nutrition* (2nd ed), Oxford: Oxford University Press.

   Munns C, Zacharin RM, Rodda PC, Batch JA, Morley R, Cranswick NE, et al 2006, *Prevention and treatment of infant and childhood vitamin D deficiency in Australia and New Zealand: a consensus statement*, The Medical Journal of Australia 185:268-272.

   World Health Organization publication 2002, *Nutrient Adequacy of Exclusive Breastfeeding*, Geneva: World Health Organization. Accessed 19/3/12 from www.who.int/nutrition/publications/infantfeeding/nut_adequacy_of_exc_bfeeding_eng.pdf

5. Kent JC 2007, *How Breastfeeding Works*, Journal of Midwifery & Women's Health 52(6):564-570.

6. Sala-Vila A, Castellote AI, Rodriguez-Palmero M, Campoy C, López-Sabater MC 2005, *Lipid composition in human breastmilk from Granada (Spain): Changes during lactation*, Nutrition 21:467-473.

7. Dietitians Association of Australia 2011, *Unsaturated fats*. Accessed 1/11/2011 from daa. asn.au/for-the-public/smart-eating-for-you/nutrition-a-z/unsaturated-fats/

CHAPTER 35

1. Berlin CM, Denson HM, Daniel CH, Ward RM 1984, *Disposition of dietary caffeine in milk, saliva, and plasma of lactating women*, Pediatrics 73(1):59-63.

2. Aranda JV, Collinge JM, Zinman R, Watters G 1979, *Maturation of caffeine elimination in infancy*, Archives of Disease in Childhood 54:946-949.

3. Liston J 1998, *Breastfeeding and the use of recreational drugs – alcohol, caffeine, nicotine and marijuana*, Breastfeeding Review 6(2):27-30.

4. Nehlig A, Debry G 1994, *Consequences on the newborn of chronic maternal consumption of coffee during gestation and lactation: a review*, Journal of the American College of Nutrition 13(1):6-21.

5. Giglia RC, Binns CW 2006, *Alcohol and lactation: a systematic review*, Nutrition and Dietetics 63:103-116.

   National Health and Medical Research Council 2012, *Infant Feeding Guidelines*, Canberra: National Health and Medical Research Council. Accessed 18/2/13 www.eatforhealth.gov.au

6. Giglia RC, Binns CW 2006, *Alcohol and lactation: a systematic review*, Nutrition and Dietetics 63:103-116.

7. Ibid.

CHAPTER 36

1. Zheng T, Jinho Y, Min Hee O, Zhou Z 2011, *The Atopic March: Progression from Atopic Dermatitis to Allergic Rhinitis and Asthma*, Allergy, Asthma and Immunology Research 3(2):67-73.

2. Waserman S, Watson W 2011, *Food allergy*, Allergy, Asthma and Clinical Immunology 7(Suppl 1):S7.

3. Vandenplas Y, Koletzko S, Isolauri E, Hill D, Oranje AP, Brueton M, et al 2007, *Guidelines for the diagnosis and management of cow's milk protein allergy in infants*, Archives of Disease in Childhood 92:902-908.

4. The Royal Children's Hospital Centre for Community Child Health 2012, *Food allergies: reducing the risk*, Community Paediatric Review 20(2):5-6.

5. Better Heath Channel 2011, *Food allergy and intolerance.* Accessed 14/12/12 from http://www.betterhealth.vic.gov.au/bhcv2/bhcarticles.nsf/pages/Food_allergy_and_intolerance

CHAPTER 37

1. Kent JC, Leon MR, Cregan MD, Ramsay DT, Doherty DA, Hartmann P 2006, *Volume and Frequency of Breastfeedings and Fat Content of Breastmilk Throughout the Day*, Pediatrics 117(3):e387-e395.

   Mitoulas LR, Kent JC, Cox DB, Owens RA, Sherriff JL, Hartmann PE 2002, *Variation in fat, lactose and protein in human milk over 24h and throughout the first year of lactation*, British Journal of Nutrition 88:29–37.

2. Heyman MB for the Committee on Nutrition 2006, *Lactose intolerance in infants, children, and adolescents*, Pediatrics 118(3):1279-1286.

3. Heyman MB for the Committee on Nutrition 2006, *Lactose intolerance in infants,*

children, and adolescents, Pediatrics 118(3):1279-1286.

4. Oddy WH 2001, *Breastfeeding protects against illness and infection in infants and children: a review of the evidence*, Breastfeeding Review 9(2):11-8.

5. Heyman MB for the Committee on Nutrition 2006, *Lactose intolerance in infants, children, and adolescents*, Pediatrics 118(3):1279-1286.

CHAPTER 38

1. Hegar B, Dewanti NR, Kadim M, Alatas S, Firmansyah A, Vandenplas Y 2009, *Natural evolution of regurgitation in healthy infants*, Acta Paediatrica 98(7):1189-1193.

2. Salvatore S, Vandenplas Y 2002, *Gastroesophageal reflux and cow milk allergy: is there a link?*, Pediatrics 110(5):972-984.

3. Arguin AL, Swartz MK 2004, *Gastroesophageal Reflux in Infants: A Primary Care Perspective*, Pediatric Nursing 30(1):45-51, 71.

4. Ibid.

5. Ibid.

6. Ibid.

7. Ibid.

8. Orenstein S, Shalaby T 1996, *Reflux symptoms in 100 normal infants: Diagnostic validity of the infant gastroesophageal reflux questionnaire*, Clinical Pediatrics 35(12):607-614.

9. Hegar B, Dewanti NR, Kadim M, Alatas S, Firmansyah A, Vandenplas Y 2009, *Natural evolution of regurgitation in healthy infants*, Acta Paediatrica 98(7):1189-1193.

10. Parrilla Rodríguez AM, Dávila Torres RR, González Méndez ME, Gorrín Peralta JJ 2002, *Knowledge about breastfeeding in mothers of infants with gastroesophageal reflux*, Puerto Rico health sciences journal 21(1):25-29.

11. Ewer AK, Durbin GM, Morgan ME, Booth IW 1994, *Gastric emptying in preterm infants*, Archives of Disease in Childhood. Fetal and Neonatal Edition 71(1):F24-F27.

12. Arguin AL, Swartz MK 2004, *Gastroesophageal Reflux in Infants: A Primary Care Perspective*, Pediatric Nursing 30(1):45-51, 71.

13. Alaswad B, Toubas PL, Grunow JE 1996, *Environmental tobacco smoke exposure and gastroesophageal reflux in infants with apparent life-threatening events*, The Journal of Oklahoma State Medical Association 89(7):233-237.

14. Horvath A, Dziechciarz P, Szajewska H 2008, *The effect of thickened-feed interventions on gastroesophageal reflux in infants: systematic review and meta-analysis of randomized, controlled trials*, Pediatrics 122(6):e1268-e1277.

15. Orenstein SR, Shalaby TM, Putnam PE 1992, *Thickened feedings as a cause of increased coughing when used as therapy for gastroesophageal reflux in infants*, The Journal of Pediatrics 121(6):913-915.

16. Mascarenhas R, Landry L, Khoshoo V 2005, *Difficulty in defecation in infants with gastroesophageal reflux treated with smaller volume feeds thickened with rice cereal*, Clinical Pediatrics 44(8):671-673.

17. World Health Organization statement 2011, *Exclusive breastfeeding for six months best for babies everywhere*, Geneva: World Health Organization. Accessed 19/2/12 from

www.who.int/mediacentre/news/statements/2011/breastfeeding_20110115/en/index.html

CHAPTER 41

1. Amir LH, Pirotta MV, Raval M 2011, *Breastfeeding - Evidence based guidelines for the use of medicines*, Australian Family Physician 40(9):684-690.

CHAPTER 42

1. Huggins K, Petok E, Mireles O 2000, *Markers of lactation insufficiency: a study of 34 mothers*, Current Issues in Clinical Lactation 25-35.

   Neifert MR, Seacat JM, Jobe WE 1985, *Lactation failure due to insufficient glandular development of the breast*, Pediatrics 76(5):823-828.

2. Markey CM, Rubin BS, Soto AM, Sonnenschein C 2003, *Endocrine disruptors: from wingspread to environmental developmental biology*, The Journal of Steroid Biochemistry and Molecular Biology 83(1-5):235-244.

3. Marasco L, Marmet C, Shell E 2000, *Polycystic ovary syndrome: a connection to insufficient milk supply?* Journal of Human Lactation 16(2):143-148.

4. Motil KJ, Thotathuchery M, Montandon CM, Hachey DL, Boutton TW, Klein PD, et al 1994, *Insulin, cortisol and thyroid hormones modulate maternal protein status and milk production and composition in humans*, The Journal of Nutrition 124(8):1248–1257.

5. Rasmussen K, Kjolhede L 2004, *Pregnant overweight and obesity diminish the prolactin response to suckling in the first week postpartum*, Pediatrics 113(5):e465-e471.

6. Arthur PG, Smith M, Hartmann PE 1989, *Milk lactose, citrate and glucose as markers of lactogenesis in normal and diabetic women*, Journal of Pediatric Gastroenterology and Nutrition 9(4):488-496.

   Arthur PG, Kent JC, Hartmann PE 1994, *Metabolites of lactose synthesis in milk from diabetic and nondiabetic women during lactogenesis II*, Journal of Pediatric Gastroenterology and Nutrition 19(1):100-108.

   Hartmann P, Cregan M 2001, *Lactogenesis and the effects of insulin-dependent diabetes mellitus and prematurity*, Journal of Human Nutrition 131(11):3016S-3020S.

7. Gei-Guardia O, Soto-Herrera E, Gei-Brealey A, Chen-Ku C 2011, *Sheehan syndrome in Costa Rica: clinical experience with 60 cases*, Endocrine Practice 17(3):337-344.

   Thompson JF, Heal LJ, Roberts CL, Ellwood DA 2010, *Women's breastfeeding experiences following a significant primary postpartum haemorrhage: a multicentre cohort study*, International Breastfeeding Journal 5:5.

   Willis C, Livingstone V 1995, *Infant insufficient milk syndrome associated with maternal postpartum hemorrhage*, Journal of Human Lactation 11(2):123-126.

8. Anderson AM 2001, *Disruption of lactogenesis by retained placental fragments*, Journal of Human Lactation 17(2):142-144.

9. West D, Marasco L 2009, *The Breastfeeding Mother's Guide to Making More Milk*, New York: McGraw Hill.

10. Andrade R, Coca K, Abrao A 2010, *Breastfeeding pattern in the first month of life in women submitted to breast reduction and augmentation*, Journal de Pediatria (Rio J) 86(3):239-244.

Michalopoulos K 2007, *The effects of breast augmentation surgery on future ability to lactate*, The Breast Journal 13(1):62-67.

Souto G, Giugliani E, Giugliani C, Schneider M 2003, *The impact of breast reduction surgery on breastfeeding performance*, Journal of Human Lactation 19(1):43-49.

Thibaudeau S, Sinno H, Williams B 2010, *The effects of breast reduction on successful breastfeeding: a systematic review*, Journal of Plastic Reconstructive and Aesthetic Surgery 63(10):1688-1693.

11. Garbin CP, Deacon JP, Rowan MK, Hartmann PE, Geddes DT 2009, *Association of Nipple Piercing With Abnormal Milk Production and Breastfeeding*, JAMA 301(24):2550-2551.

12. Faculty of Sexual and Reproductive Healthcare Clinical Effectiveness Unit 2009, *FSRH guidance postnatal sexual and reproductive health*. Accessed 18/2/12 from www.fsrh.org/pdfs/CEUGuidancePostnatal09.pdf

West D, Marasco L 2009, *The Breastfeeding Mother's Guide to Making More Milk*, New York: McGraw Hill.

13. West D, Marasco L 2009, *The Breastfeeding Mother's Guide to Making More Milk*, New York: McGraw Hill.

14. Kennedy K 2010, *Fertility, Sexuality, and Contraception During Lactation* (Chapter 21). In Riordan J & Wambach K (Eds), Breastfeeding and human lactation (4th ed), Sudbury: Jones and Bartlett Publishers.

15. Aljazaf K, Hale TW, Ilett KF, Hartmann PE, Mitoulas LR, Kristensen JH, et al 2003, *Pseudoephedrine: effects on milk production in women and estimation of infant exposure via breastmilk*, British Journal of Clinical Pharmacology 56(1):18-24.

European Multicentre Study Group for Cabergoline in Lactation Inhibition 1991, *Single dose cabergoline versus bromocriptine in inhibition of puerperal lactation: randomised, double blind, multicentre study*, BMJ 302(6789):1367-1371.

16. West D, Marasco L 2009, *The Breastfeeding Mother's Guide to Making More Milk*, New York: McGraw Hill.

CHAPTER 43

1. Kent J, Mitoulas L, Cox D, Owens R, Hartmann P 1999, *Breast volume and milk production during extended lactation in women*, Experimental Physiology 84:435-447.

2. Newman J, Pitman T 2006, *The Latch: and other keys to breastfeeding success*, Texas: Hale Publishing.

Ozkan H, Tuzun F, Kumral A, Yesilirmak D, Duman N 2008, *Increased sleep tendency in jaundiced infants: role of endogenous CO*, Medical Hypotheses 71(6):879-880.

3. Riordan J, Hoover K 2010, *Perinatal and Intrapartum Care* (Chapter 7). In Riordan J & Wambach K (Eds), *Breastfeeding and human lactation* (4th ed), Sudbury: Jones and Bartlett Publishers.

4. Newman J, Pitman T 2006, *The Latch: and other keys to breastfeeding success*, Texas: Hale Publishing.

Smillie C 2010, *The Non-latching Infant*, Audio podcast from Dr Anne's Audio Player. Accessed 13/11/11 from http://www.anneeglash.com/audio/

5. Geddes DT, Kent JC, Mitoulas LR, Hartmann PE 2008, *Tongue movement and intra-oral vacuum in breastfeeding infants*, Early Human Development 84(7):471-477.

6. Fetherston CM, Lai CT, Hartmann PE 2006, *Relationships between symptoms and changes in breast physiology during lactation mastitis*, Breastfeeding Medicine 1(3):136-145.

   Hartmann PE, Prosser CG 1982, *Acute changes in the composition of milk during the ovulatory menstrual cycle in lactating women*, The Journal of Physiology 324:21-30.

CHAPTER 45

1. International Lactation Consultant Association 2005, *Clinical Guidelines for the Establishment of Exclusive breastfeeding*, Raleigh, North Carolina.

2. Shrago LC, Reifsnider E, Insel K 2006, *The Neonatal Bowel Output Study: indicators of adequate breast milk intake in neonates*, Pediatric Nursing 32(3):195-201.

3. Gartner LM et al 2005, *Breastfeeding and the use of human milk*, Pediatrics 115(2):496-506

   Yaseen H, Salem M, Darwich M 2004, *Clinical presentation of hypernatremic dehydration in exclusively breast-fed neonates*, Indian Journal of Pediatrics 71(12):1059-1062.

CHAPTER 46

1. Tunc V, Camurdan A, Ilhan M, Sahin F, Beyazova U 2008, *Factors associated with defecation patterns in 0-24-month-old children*, European Journal of Pediatrics 167(12):1357-1362.

2. International Lactation Consultant Association 2005, *Clinical Guidelines for the Establishment of Exclusive breastfeeding*, Raleigh, North Carolina.

CHAPTER 48

1. Riordan J, Hoover K 2010, *Perinatal and Intrapartum Care* (Chapter 7). In Riordan J & Wambach K (Eds), *Breastfeeding and human lactation* (4th ed), Sudbury: Jones and Bartlett Publishers.

CHAPTER 50

1. National Health and Medical Research Council 2012, *Infant Feeding Guidelines*, Canberra: National Health and Medical Research Council. Accessed 18/2/13 www.eatforhealth.gov.au

2. Noel-Weiss J, Woodend AK, Peterson WE, Gibb W, Groll DL 2011, *An observational study of associations among maternal fluids during parturition, neonatal output, and breastfed newborn*, International Breastfeeding Journal 6:9.

3. National Health and Medical Research Council 2012, *Infant Feeding Guidelines*, Canberra: National Health and Medical Research Council. Accessed 18/2/13 www.eatforhealth.gov.au

4. Ibid.

5. Ibid

6. World Health Organization Child Growth Standards 2006, Geneva: World Health Organization. Accessed 25/5/12 www.who.int/childgrowth/en/

7. Ibid.

CHAPTER 51

1. National Health and Medical Research Council 2012, *Infant Feeding Guidelines*, Canberra: National Health and Medical Research Council. Accessed 18/2/13 www.eatforhealth.gov.au

2. Ibid.

3. Ibid.

CHAPTER 52

1. Davies DP, Williams T 1983, *Is weighing babies in clinics worthwhile?* British Medical Journal 286(6368):860-863.

2. British Columbia World Health Organization Growth Standards Training material 2011. Accessed 24/4/12 from datafind.gov.bc.ca/query.html?qt=WHO+growth+training&charset=utf-8&style=health&col=qlinks&col=nrmweb&col=blogs&col=bcgovt&col=govdaily

   National Health and Medical Research Council 2003, *Dietary Guidelines for all Australians incorporating the Infant Feeding Guidelines for Health Workers.* Accessed 25/5/12 from www.nhmrc.gov.au/_files_nhmrc/publications/attachments/n34.pdf

   World Health Organization publication 2009, *Infant and young child feeding: model chapter for textbooks for medical students and allied health professionals*, Geneva: World Health Organization. Accessed 24/4/12 from whqlibdoc.who.int/publications/2009/9789241597494_eng.pdf

3. British Columbia World Health Organization Growth Standards Training material 2011. Accessed 24/4/12 from datafind.gov.bc.ca/query.html?qt=WHO+growth+training&charset=utf-8&style=health&col=qlinks&col=nrmweb&col=blogs&col=bcgovt&col=govdaily

   National Health and Medical Research Council 2012, *Infant Feeding Guidelines*, Canberra: National Health and Medical Research Council. Accessed 18/2/13 from www.eatforhealth.gov.au

   World Health Organization publication 2009, *Infant and young child feeding: model chapter for textbooks for medical students and allied health professionals*, Geneva: World Health Organization. Accessed 24/4/12 from whqlibdoc.who.int/publications/2009/9789241597494_eng.pdf

4. Ibid.

5. Ibid.

CHAPTER 57

1. Morton J, Hall JY, Wong RJ, Thairu L, Benitz WE, Rhine WD 2009, *Combining hand techniques with electric pumping increases milk production in mothers of preterm infants*, Journal of Perinatology 29(11):757-764.

CHAPTER 58

1. Neville MC, Keller R, Seacat J, Lutes V, Neifert M, Casey C, et al 1988, *Studies in human lactation: milk volumes in lactating women during the onset of lactation and full lactation*, American Society for Nutrition 48:1375-1386.

    Saint L, Smith M, Hartmann P 1984, *The yield and nutrient content of colostrum and milk from giving birth to 1 month postpartum*, British Journal of Nutrition 52:87-95.

2. Kent JC, Leon MR, Cregan MD, Ramsay DT, Doherty DA, Hartmann PE 2006, *Volume and Frequency of Breastfeedings and Fat Content of Breastmilk Throughout the Day*, Pediatrics 117(3):e387-e395.

CHAPTER 61

1. Gerritsen J, Smidt H, Rijkers GT, de Vos WM 2011, *Intestinal microbiota in human health and disease: the impact of probiotics*, Genes and Nutrition 6(3):209-240.

2. Marsha Walker, *Supplementation of the Breastfed Baby "Just One Bottle Won't Hurt" – or Will It?* Accessed 12/6/12 from www.health-e-learning.com/articles/JustOneBottle.pdf

3. Ibid.

4. Ibid.

5. Marsha Walker, *Supplementation of the Breastfed Baby "Just One Bottle Won't Hurt" – or Will It?* Accessed 12/6/12 from www.health-e-learning.com/articles/JustOneBottle.pdf

   Schurr P, Perkins EM 2008, *The relationship between feeding and necrotizing enterocolitis in very low birth weight infants*, Neonatal Network 27(6):397-407.

   Quigley MA, Henderson G, Anthony MY, McGuire W 2007, *Formula milk versus donor breastmilk for feeding preterm or low birth weight infants*, Cochrane Database System Review 17;(4):CD002971.

6. Cox SG 2006, *Expressing and storing colostrum antenatally for use in the newborn period.* Breastfeeding Review 14(3):11-16.

   Marsha Walker, *Supplementation of the Breastfed Baby "Just One Bottle Won't Hurt" – or Will It?* Accessed 12/6/12 from www.health-e-learning.com/articles/JustOneBottle.pdf

7. Cox SG 2010, *An ethical dilemma: should recommending antenatal expressing and storing of colostrum continue?* Breastfeeding Review 18(3):5-7.

   Marsha Walker, *Supplementation of the Breastfed Baby "Just One Bottle Won't Hurt" – or Will It?* Accessed 12/6/12 from www.health-e-learning.com/articles/JustOneBottle.pdf

8. Cox SG 2006, *Expressing and storing colostrum antenatally for use in the newborn period.* Breastfeeding Review 14(3):11-16.

   Cox SG 2010, *An ethical dilemma: should recommending antenatal expressing and storing of colostrum continue?* Breastfeeding Review 18(3):5-7.

   Marsha Walker, *Supplementation of the Breastfed Baby "Just One Bottle Won't Hurt" – or Will It?* Accessed 12/6/12 from www.health-e-learning.com/articles/JustOneBottle.pdf

9. Marsha Walker, *Supplementation of the Breastfed Baby "Just One Bottle Won't Hurt" – or Will It?* Accessed 12/6/12 from www.health-e-learning.com/articles/JustOneBottle.pdf

CHAPTER 62

1. The Academy of Breastfeeding Medicine Protocol Committee 2010, *ABM Clinical Protocol #8: Human Milk Storage Information for Home Use for Full-Term Infants*, Breastfeeding Medicine 5(3):127-130.

2. Lawrence RA 1999, *Storage of human milk and the influence of procedures on immunological components of human milk*, Acta Paediatrica Supplement 88(430):14-18.

CHAPTER 63

1. Wong MM, Brower KJ, Zucker RA 2010, *Childhood sleep problems, response inhibition, and alcohol and drug outcomes in adolescence and young adulthood*, Alcoholism: Clinical and Experimental Research 4(6):1033-1044.

2. Halbower AC, Marcus CL 2003, *Sleep disorders in children.* Current Opinion in Pulmonary Medicine 9(6):471-476.

3. Ibid.

4. Wong MM, Brower KJ, Zucker RA 2010, *Childhood sleep problems, response inhibition, and alcohol and drug outcomes in adolescence and young adulthood*, Alcoholism: Clinical and Experimental Research 4(6):1033-1044.

5. Landhuis CE, Poulton R, Welch D, Hancox RJ 2008 , *Childhood Sleep Time and Long-Term Risk for Obesity: A 32-Year Prospective Birth Cohort Study*, Pediatrics 122(5):955-960.

6. Hill CM, Hogan AM, Karmiloff-Smith A 2007, *To sleep, perchance to enrich learning?* Archives of Disease in Childhood 92(7):637-643.

   Kopasz M, Loessl B, Hornyak M, Riemann D, Nissen C, Piosczyk H, et al 2010, *Sleep and memory in healthy children and adolescents - a critical review*, Sleep Medicine Reviews 14(3):167-177.

7. Rivkees SA 2003, *Developing circadian rhythmicity in infants*, Pediatrics 112(2):373-381.

8. Ferber SG, Laudon M, Kuint J, Weller A, Zisapel N 2002, *Massage therapy by mothers enhances the adjustment of circadian rhythms to the nocturnal period in full-term infants*, Journal of Developmental and Behavioral Pediatrics 23(6):410-415.

   McMillen IC, Kok JS, Adamson TM, Deayton JM, Nowak R 1991, *Development of circadian sleep-wake rhythms in preterm and full-term infants*, Pediatric Research 29(4 Pt 1):381-384.

9. Cubero J, Valero V, Sánchez J, Rivero M, Parvez H, Rodríguez AB, et al 2005, *The circadian rhythm of tryptophan in breastmilk affects the rhythms of 6-sulfatoxymelatonin and sleep in newborn*, Neuro Endocrinology Letters 26(6):657-661.

10. Kulkarni A, Kaushik JS, Gupta P, Sharma H, Agrawal RK 2010, *Massage and touch therapy in neonates: the current evidence*, Indian Pediatrics 47(9):771-776.

11. Ferber SG, Laudon M, Kuint J, Weller A, Zisapel N 2002, *Massage therapy by mothers enhances the adjustment of circadian rhythms to the nocturnal period in full-term infants*, Journal of Developmental and Behavioral Pediatrics 23(6):410-415.

12. Harrison Y 2004, *The relationship between daytime exposure to light and night-time sleep in 6-12-week-old infants*, Journal of Sleep Research 13(4):345-352.

CHAPTER 64

1. Uvnäs-Moberg K, Marchini G, Winberg J 1993, *Plasma cholecystokinin concentrations after breast feeding in healthy 4 day old infants*, Archives of Disease in Childhood 68(1):46-48.

2. Doan T, Gardiner A, Gay CL, Lee KA 2007, *Breast-feeding increases sleep duration of new parents*, Journal of Perinatal Neonatal Nursing 21(3):200-206.

3. Blyton DM, Sullivan CE, Edwards N 2002, *Lactation is associated with an increase in slow-wave sleep in women*, Journal of Sleep Research 11(4):297-303.

4. Doan T, Gardiner A, Gay CL, Lee KA 2007, *Breast-feeding increases sleep duration of new parents*, Journal of Perinatal Neonatal Nursing 21(3):200-206.

CHAPTER 65

1. van Sleuwen BE, Engelberts AC, Boere-Boonekamp MM, Kuis W, Schulpen TW, L'Hoir MP 2007, *Swaddling: a systematic review*, Pediatrics 120(4):e1097-e1106.

CHAPTER 66

1. Sids and Kids, *Safe Sleeping*. Accessed 17/3/12 from www.sidsandkids.org/safe-sleeping/

2. Ibid.

3. Scragg RK, Mitchell EA, Stewart AW, Ford RPK, Taylor BJ, Hassall IB, et al 1996, *Infant room-sharing and prone sleep position in sudden infant death syndrome*, Lancet 347(8993):7-12.

4. Hauck FR, Thompson JM, Tanabe KO, Moon RY, Vennemann MM 2011, *Breastfeeding and reduced risk of sudden infant death syndrome: a meta-analysis*, Pediatrics 128(1):103-110.

CHAPTER 67

1. Davis KF, Parker KP, Montgomery GL 2004, *Sleep in infants and young children: Part one: normal sleep*, Journal of Pediatric Health Care 8(2):65-71.

   Iglowsten I, Jenni OG, Molinari L, Largo RH 2003, *Sleep duration from infancy to adolescence: Reference values and generational trends*, Pediatrics 111:2, 302-307.

2. Davis KF, Parker KP, Montgomery GL 2004, *Sleep in infants and young children: Part one: normal sleep*, Journal of Pediatric Health Care 8(2):65-71.

   Iglowsten I, Jenni OG, Molinari L, Largo RH 2003, *Sleep duration from infancy to adolescence: Reference values and generational trends*, Pediatrics 111:2, 302-307.

3. Iglowsten I, Jenni OG, Molinari L, Largo RH 2003, *Sleep duration from infancy to adolescence: Reference values and generational trends*, Pediatrics 111:2, 302-307.

CHAPTER 68

1. Davis KF, Parker KP, Montgomery GL 2004, *Sleep in infants and young children: Part one: normal sleep*, Journal of Pediatric Health Care 8(2):65-71.

   Sadeh A 2001, *Sleeping Like a Baby*, New Haven and London: Yale University Press.

2. Adamson M, Davey M, Cranage S 2001, *26 Facts about Sleep and Your Baby*, Clayton, Melbourne: Melbourne Children's Sleep Unit, Department of Paediatrics, Monash University.

   Davis KF, Parker KP, Montgomery GL 2004, *Sleep in infants and young children: Part one: normal sleep*, Journal of Pediatric Health Care 8(2):65-71.

3. Davis KF, Parker KP, Montgomery GL 2004, *Sleep in infants and young children: Part one: normal sleep*, Journal of Pediatric Health Care 8(2):65-71.

4. Davis KF, Parker KP, Montgomery GL 2004, *Sleep in infants and young children: Part one: normal sleep*, Journal of Pediatric Health Care 8(2):65-71.

March of Dimes 2003, *Perinatal Nursing Education, Understanding the Behavior of Term Infants*. Accessed 17/3/12 from www.marchofdimes.com/nursing/modnemedia/othermedia/states.pdf

5. Ibid.

6. Davis KF, Parker KP, Montgomery GL 2004, *Sleep in infants and young children: Part one: normal sleep*, Journal of Pediatric Health Care 8(2):65-71.

7. Ibid.

8. Ibid.

CHAPTER 69

1. Iglowsten I, Jenni OG, Molinari L, Largo RH 2003, *Sleep duration from infancy to adolescence: Reference values and generational trends*, Pediatrics 111:2, 302-307.

CHAPTER 72

1. Douglas PS, Hiscock H 2010, *The unsettled baby: crying out for an integrated, multidisciplinary primary care approach*, The Medical Journal of Australia 193(9):533-536.

   National Health and Medical Research Council 2012, *Infant Feeding Guidelines*, Canberra: National Health and Medical Research Council. Accessed 18/2/13 from www.eatforhealth.gov.au

2. Ibid.

3. McKenna J 2008, *Biological Imperatives and Mother-Infant Co-sleeping: Why Human Babies Do Not and Should Not Sleep Alone*, Neuroanthropology Website. Accessed 13/2/2012 from neuroanthropology.net/2008/12/21/cosleeping-and-biological-imperatives-why-human-babies-do-not-and-should-not-sleep-alone/

4. Ibid.

CHAPTER 73

1. Sids and Kids, *Safe Sleeping*. Accessed 17/3/12 from www.sidsandkids.org/safe-sleeping/

2. Ball HL, Hooker E, Kelly PJ 2000, *Parent-infant co-sleeping: fathers' roles and perspectives*, Infant and Child Development 9:67-74.

   Rigda RS, McMillen IC, Buckley P 2000, *Bed sharing patterns in a cohort of Australian infants during the first six months after birth*, Journal of Paediatrics and Child Health 36:117-121.

3. McKenna JJ, McDade T 2005, *Why babies should never sleep alone: a review of the co-sleeping controversy in relation to SIDS, bedsharing and breast feeding*, Paediatric Respiratory Reviews 6(2):134-52.

   UNICEF UK 2011, *Caring for your baby at night* (Leaflet). Accessed 17/3/12 from www.unicef.org.uk/BabyFriendly/Resources/Resources-for-parents/Caring-for-your-baby-at-night/

4. Blair PS, Fleming PJ, Smith IJ, Ward Platt M, Young J, Nadin P, et al 1999, *Babies sleeping with parents: case-control study of factors influencing the risk of the sudden infant death syndrome*, British Medical Journal 319:1457-1461.

   Byard RW, Beal S, Blackbourne B, Nadeau JM, Krous HDF 2001, *Specific dangers associated with infants sleeping on sofas*, Journal of Paediatric Child Health 37:476-478.

Carpenter RG, Irgens LM, Blair PS, England PD, Fleming P, Huber J, Jorch G, Schreuder P 2004, *Sudden unexplained infant death in 20 regions in Europe: case control study*, Lancet 363:185-191.

Hauck FR, Herman SM, Donovan M, Lyasu S, Moore C, Donoghue E, et al 2003, *Sleep environment and the risk of sudden infant death syndrome in an urban population: The Chicago Infant Mortality Study*, Pediatrics 111(5):1207-1214.

McKenna J 2012, *Safe Cosleeping Guidelines*. Accessed 17/3/12 from www.cosleeping. nd.edu/safe-co-sleeping-guidelines/

Scragg R, Mitchell EA, Taylor BJ, Stewart AW, Ford RPK, Thompson J, et al 1993, *Bed sharing, smoking, and alcohol in the sudden infant death syndrome*, British Medical Journal 307:1312-1318.

UNICEF UK 2011, *Caring for your baby at night* (Leaflet). Accessed 17/3/12 from www. unicef.org.uk/BabyFriendly/Resources/Resources-for-parents/Caring-for-your-baby-at-night/

Vennemann MM, Hense HW, Bajanowski T, Blair PS, Complojer C, Moon RY, et al 2012, *Bed Sharing and the risk of sudden infant death syndrome: can we resolve the debate?* Pediatrics 160(1):44-48.e2.

CHAPTER 74

1. World Health Organization publication 2009, *Infant and young child feeding: model chapter for textbooks for medical students and allied health professionals*, Geneva: World Health Organization. Accessed 24/5/12 from whqlibdoc.who.int/publications/2009/9789241597494_eng.pdf

2. van de Ritj H, Plooij F 2010, *The Wonder Weeks*, Kiddy World Promotions BV, The Netherlands.

Index